Environmental Evaluation: Perception and Public Policy

Environmental Evaluation: Perception and Public Policy

ERVIN H. ZUBE
University of Arizona

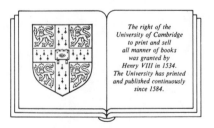

The right of the
University of Cambridge
to print and sell
all manner of books
was granted by
Henry VIII in 1534.
The University has printed
and published continuously
since 1584.

CAMBRIDGE UNIVERSITY PRESS

Cambridge
London   New York   New Rochelle
Melbourne   Sydney

To Margaret and Rick

Published by the Press Syndicate of the University of Cambridge
The Pitt Building, Trumpington Street, Cambridge CB2 1RP
32 East 57th Street, New York, NY 10022, USA
296 Beaconsfield Parade, Middle Park, Melbourne 3206, Australia

First published 1980 by Wadsworth, Inc.
First published by Cambridge University Press 1984

Printed in the United States of America

ISBN 0 521 31972 2

SERIES FOREWORD

The study of environment and behavior has shown a rapid development in recent decades; we expect that interest in this field will continue at a high level in the future. As a young and informative area, it has many exciting qualities. For example, the analysis of the relationship between human behavior and the physical environment has attracted researchers from many fields in the *social sciences,* such as psychology, sociology, geography, and anthropology, and from the *environmental design* fields, such as architecture, urban and regional planning, and interior design. The multidisciplinary character of this field has led to an atmosphere of stimulation, cross-fertilization, and, yes, even confusion and difficulty in communication. Furthermore, because of the diversity in intellectual styles and goals of its participants, research on environment and behavior has as often dealt with applied, real-world problems of environmental design as it has treated basic and theoretical issues.

These factors, coupled with the relatively young stage of development of the field, led us to believe that a series of short books on different areas of the environment and behavior field would be useful to students, researchers, and practitioners. Our view was that the study of environment and behavior had not yet firmed up to the point that a single volume would do justice to the wide range of topics now being studied or to the variety of audiences interested in the field. Furthermore, it became clear to us that new topical areas have emerged over the past decade and that some vehicle is necessary to facilitate the evolutionary growth of the field.

For these reasons, Brooks/Cole established the present series of books on environment and behavior with the following goals in mind: first, we endeavored to develop a series of short volumes on areas of research and knowledge that are relatively well established and are characterized by a reasonably substantial body of knowledge. Second, we have recruited authors from a diversity of disciplines who bring to bear a variety of perspectives on various subjects in the field. Third, we asked authors not only to summarize research and knowledge on their topic but also to set forth a ''point of view,'' if not a theoretical orientation, in their book. It was our intention, therefore, that these volumes be more than textbooks in the usual sense of the term—that they not only summarize existing knowledge in an understandable way but also, we hope, advance the field intellectually. Fourth, we wanted the books in the series to be useful to a broad range of students and readers. We planned for the volumes to be educationally valuable to students and professionals from different fields in the social sciences and environmental-design fields and to be of interest to readers with different levels of formal professional training. As part of our broad and flexible strategy, the series will allow instructors in a variety of fields teaching a variety of courses to select different combinations of volumes to meet their particular course needs. In so doing, an instructor might select several books for a course or use a small number of volumes as supplementary reading material.

Because the series is open-ended and not restricted to a particular body of content, we hope that it will not only serve to summarize knowledge in the field of environment and behavior but also contribute to the growth and development of this exciting area of study.

Irwin Altman
Daniel Stokols
Lawrence S. Wrightsman

PREFACE

This book deals with environmental quality—a topic that captured public attention in the 1960s and is a matter of continuing concern to both public officials and private citizens. Specifically, this book focuses on a qualitative evaluation of the environment based on the perceptions and experiences of the users of the environment. The relationships between users' perceptions and experiences and the laws, executive orders, and administrative directives issued in the name of environmental quality are explored, along with the relationships between users' perceptions and experiences and environmental planning, design, and management.

Environmental Evaluation is intended for use by students of the social and behavioral sciences and by the planning, design, and management professions. It is an introduction to user-based environmental evaluation—a rapidly developing area in applied behavioral science.

Chapters 1–4 describe the context within which the evaluation process occurs. Chapter 1 introduces major themes and issues. It provides a general introduction to the idea of user-based environmental evaluation, further definitions of terms and concepts used in the book, and an organizational schema for the conduct or analysis of evaluation studies. The schema provides a framework for the presentation and discussion of the case studies in Chapter 5, 6, and 7.

The evolution of environmental policy in the U.S. from resource exploitation to consumer orientation is reviewed in Chapter 2. The current emphasis on consumer orientation in public policy, which provides a more supportive climate for user-based evaluations among government agencies and professionals, is also discussed in Chapter 2. Chapter 3 addresses some of the reasons for the gap between possibilities for user-based evaluations and actual practices. The state of the art in environmental-perception research also is briefly reviewed.

The process of planning, designing, and managing the environment is the topic of Chapter 4. Attention is directed to the iterative nature of the process and to means of accommodating the consumer-orientation or public-participation mandates of current policies. Three stages in the process are identified as particularly important for the inclusion of user-based evaluations. First is the inventory stage—the evaluation of existing environments. Second is the evaluation of future environments—the alternatives' stage when, for example, a choice is to be made among several plans, designs, or management strategies for implementation. The third stage, the evaluation of new or modified environments, occurs after implementation—after the plan, design, or management strategy has been implemented and users have had a reasonable opportunity to experience the new or modified environment.

The second half of this book is organized around examples of actual environmental evaluations and employs a case-study approach. Chapter 5 includes evaluation studies of existing environments, or, as indicated in Chapter 4, examples from the inventory stage of the planning, design, and management process. Chapter 6 is concerned with the evaluation of future environments. Cases are presented that involve problems of communicating or simulating the essence of possible alternative futures and of evaluating such simulations. Chapter 7 presents postconstruction evaluation studies, including case studies of single projects, and a comparative evaluation of multiple projects.

Finally, Chapter 8 reviews and summarizes the salient problems and issues raised in the case studies presented in the preceding chapters. Primary emphases are on the design of evaluation studies, methods used, and utility of the information obtained.

Writing a book is both a solitary and a shared activity. Final responsibility for the concepts and issues and for the way in which they are organized and communicated must rest with the author; however, every author is indebted to a host of colleagues, and in my case this includes students who have helped to shape concepts and define issues. Their questions, suggestions, and collaboration in research projects have influenced the way in which I have organized the material in this book.

During twelve years of professional, academic, and research activity in the area of environmental evaluation I have had the good fortune of sharing responsibilities for graduate seminars at the University of Massachusetts with Julius Gy Fabos, Arnold Friedmann, D. Geoffrey Hayward, and Stanley Moss, each of whom has had an influence on the ideas presented in this book. There have also been many graduate students from a wide range of disciplines, including art, landscape architecture, interior design, psychology, regional planning, and sociology, who have questioned and debated the topic of environmental evaluation both in and out of the classroom. I owe much to these students.

The case studies used in this book draw on the work of a number of individuals who provided background information, assisted in obtaining access to illustrations, and reviewed drafts of the case studies—my thanks to Donald Appleyard, Clare Cooper, Rachel Kaplan, and Ewing Miller for assistance with the City Streets, Easter Hill Village, City Park, and Building Form studies respectively. I am indebted to Craig Zimring and Christopher Knight, who not only assisted in the securing of materials for the Belchertown State School study but also provided critical reviews of early drafts of several chapters.

I was personally involved in three of the case studies: as a member of the professional seminar that studied the aesthetic enhancement of Niagara Falls; as the principal investigator for the evaluation of National Park Service visitor centers; and as principal consultant to the Virgin Islands Planning Office for Coastal Zone Management and development of the household survey. The contributions of Joseph Crystal and James Palmer, my colleagues on the Visitor Center study, were considerable indeed. My thanks to them. And, to my colleagues in the Virgin Islands Planning Office, Darlan Brin, Ed Lindelof, and in particular, Marsha McLaughlin—thank you.

I want to express my thanks to the editors for this series of books published by Brooks/Cole—Irwin Altman, Dan Stockols, and Larry Wrightsman—and to William Hicks, managing editor. I thank them for their invitation to write this book and for their critical and helpful reviews of early drafts of the manuscript.

Finally, my deep appreciation to Margaret Zube for being my best critic and for providing the essential supportive environment.

Ervin H. Zube

CONTENTS

Chapter 1

EVALUATING ENVIRONMENTS

WHY EVALUATE ENVIRONMENTS?

Evaluation studies are intended to provide valid, reliable, and useful information to those who manage the environment, who promulgate and implement policy, and who plan and design the environment. In other words, evaluation studies are intended to provide information to improve the quality of decision making with reference to environmental management as well as to change and modification.

The Seventh Annual Report of the Council on Environmental Quality (1978) reports a predicted population growth for the United States of 47 million people, to a total of 262 million by the year 2000. Three major spatial patterns of growth are also reported. The first two, continued growth of major metropolitan areas and a shift from the northeast and north-central sections of the country to the south and west sections have been recognized for some time. The third pattern, however, represents a reversal of an historic growth pattern and a very recent phenomenon—the growth of nonmetropolitan counties at a rate faster than that of metropolitan counties. This is a reversal of a pattern that had continued almost without interruption from the first national census in 1790 to the census of 1970. The environmental effects of this changing pattern are not always clear or easy to predict. Monitoring of change and assessment of related impacts, however, can provide information relevant to the promulgation of land-use policies that will guide change along more rational lines in consonance with accepted standards and criteria for a quality environment.

Wherever growth occurs, modification of the environment will occur, sometimes under the aegis of federal, state, or local policies relating to housing, recreation, transportation, and the like. Evaluation studies provide a means for assessing the efficacy of those policies as evidenced by the success or failure of the subdivisions, apartments, parks, playgrounds, and subway stations that result from their implementation. Such studies can provide the kind of information that makes it possible to modify, fine-tune, or abandon old policies or to develop new policies. They provide information based on empirical data rather than on guesses and intuition.

1

Evaluation of existing environments provides insights into variations in the quality of different environments—for example, housing, parks, and schools—at different times and in different places. It helps to identify and specify emerging problems and societal needs previously ignored or misunderstood. It can help identify the adequacy of existing environments, point the way to their renovation and rehabilitation, and provide an empirical basis for the promulgation and implementation of new approaches to environmental planning, management, and design. In other words, information obtained from evaluation studies contributes to the making of better decisions by designers, planners, and policymakers. It provides feedback, systematic learning from past experience, and guidance for the future.

OF VALUES AND EVALUATION

We all evaluate these environments when making a judgment, consciously or unconsciously, about which house or apartment to live in, which beach to visit on a hot summer day, or which route to travel to and from school or employment. We seek out environments we believe to be most supportive of our anticipated activities and most suitable for satisfying our personal needs. These judgments are influenced not only by perceptions of the physical environment, but also by a host of extra-environmental concerns and characteristics, including available money for housing, length of visit to the beach, time allotted for travel to and from work or school, past experiences, aspirations for the future, marital and family status, life style, and social status. The importance of various physical environmental characteristics and extraenvironmental factors may be consciously considered and weighed in making some decisions, while other decisions may appear impulsive, if not irrational. Each decision, however, involves identifying a specific domain of the physical environment related to the resolution of a problem or the satisfaction of a personal need and the invoking of standards or criteria that facilitate evaluation. And each evaluation is accomplished by making comparisons among alternative environments.

For example, a college student looking for housing may have several options, including two or three different campus dormitory accommodations (a single or double room or a suite) and two or three private apartment complexes near the campus. A number of concerns may influence the decision as to which alternative will provide the most satisfying housing: size of rooms, architectural style, state of repair and quality of maintenance, opportunities for privacy from both roommates and neighbors, kinds of neighbors (students, working singles, families with children), availability of a dining hall as opposed to meal preparation in an apartment, convenience to classes and library, opportunities to share responsibilities for cooking and cleaning among two to four roommates, greater or lesser freedom to entertain friends, and costs for food and rent.

A student engaged in making this decision is conducting an inventory of existing environments, assessing each alternative, implicitly or explicitly, against a set of personally important physical, social, and economic criteria, and then selecting that alternative judged to provide the most satisfying accommodation. This is a highly personal evaluation for an individual need.

If the college is contemplating the construction of new student housing or the renovation of existing dormitories, a process very similar to that followed by the individual student might be designed to provide guidance for revising housing policy and formulating designs for the future. Collecting the evaluative judgments of a representative sample of students, in order to profile student satisfaction and dissatisfaction with a cross-section of existing dormitories and apartments, could help to identify those physical, social, and economic aspects of housing most important to different sectors of the student population. Such an approach to evaluation could provide the college with important information on the characteristics of the most successful existing housing, why certain forms of housing are perceived as more satisfactory than others, and the relative importance of various housing elements at different rental rates—elements such as social rooms in dormitories, individual rooms, suite arrangements, and location on the campus. This kind of aggregate user-evaluation is the primary focus of this book.

The process of evaluation relates to the determination of the quality or worth of the environment. It requires that the environment be measured in reference to some standard of comparison. Units of measurement can be derived by using physical instruments such as yardsticks, decibel meters, and chemical analysis, or they can be derived using the human perceptual system as a measuring instrument. One component of a quality library environment may be the sound level, which can be measured by using a decibel meter or by asking library users whether the sound level is too high, too low, or all right for studying and whether the quality of the sound (for example, the pitch) affects studying. The decibel meter readings can be compared to sound level standards derived from numerous library situations, in the context of professional judgments as to acceptable sound levels. The students' responses, however, are probably influenced by previous experiences in other libraries (an experiential standard of comparison) and by expectations in the present library.

Evaluation is also related to the concept of values, that abstract frame of reference encompassing beliefs, thoughts, feelings, and attitudes that influence judgments, setting of goals, identification of needs, and discrimination among competing demands. Values are essential antecedents to evaluation, since they help specify needs and problems and constitute a starting point in the evaluative process (Sochman, 1967).

Figure 1–1 depicts, in simplified form, components of an aggregate or user-based evaluation process that defines values, needs, and problems within the context of contemporary environmental values. Public policy, as discussed in

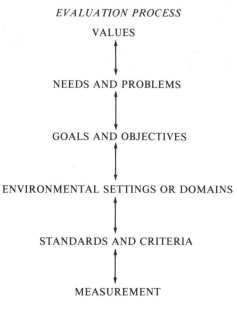

EVALUATION PROCESS

VALUES

↕

NEEDS AND PROBLEMS

↕

GOALS AND OBJECTIVES

↕

ENVIRONMENTAL SETTINGS OR DOMAINS

↕

STANDARDS AND CRITERIA

↕

MEASUREMENT

Figure 1–1

Chapter 2, is an important medium for the explication of such values. For example, the National Environmental Policy Act of 1969 (NEPA) states:

> The purposes of this Act are: to declare a national policy which will encourage a productive and enjoyable harmony between man and his environment; to promote efforts which will prevent or eliminate damage to the environment and biosphere and stimulate the health and welfare of man; to enrich the understanding of the ecological systems and natural resources important to the nation. . . .

This is a broad and important, albeit abstract statement of national values as set forth by Congress and signed by the President. It speaks to broadly defined environmental problems and societal needs. Obviously, it also requires considerable specification and detailing to be transformed into programs and projects that can be implemented in support of the value placed on a harmonious user-environment relationship. Nevertheless, it points the direction to the identification of more specific goals or societal objectives relating to health, safety, satisfaction, productive ecosystems, and environmental protection. It also points the direction to the identification of the environmental settings or domains related to the goals and objectives.

The previously cited case of a college considering the construction of new housing or the renovation of existing facilities provides a useful example with which to trace the several steps in the evaluation process outlined in Figure 1–1. The need is student housing. This value is well documented in the federal, state, and local policies adopted to facilitate and strengthen higher education in universities, colleges, and junior colleges.

The goals and objectives for student housing will be in large part dependent on the nature of the institution—public or private, predominantly residential or commuter, urban or rural, single sex or coeducational, large or small. The nature of the institution will also determine and be determined by the kinds of students who attend—whether they come from wealthy, middle-class, or poor families, whether they are first-generation college students or come from families where higher education has been a tradition for several generations, and whether they have rural or urban backgrounds.

Such factors and others will help to define the college housing goals and objectives. A large public coeducational college in a rural area may include among its housing goals (1) to provide housing supportive of the intellectual and social activities of the residents; (2) to provide housing convenient to classrooms, library, and intramural athletic facilities; (3) to provide a range of housing alternatives; and (4) to provide housing at rental rates within the economic means of all students. Specific housing objectives would interpret these abstract goals in more precise terms. For example, housing supportive of intellectual and social activities may be specified in terms of the kinds of functional spaces to be provided—game rooms, study rooms, and snack bars. Convenience may be specified in terms of travel time (for example, the objective may be to locate student housing so that all students are within fifteen minutes' access time to all points of the campus). The goal of providing a range of housing options may be restated as an objective to provide varying percentages of single occupancy rooms, double occupancy rooms, and suites, and also to provide both dormitories and residential colleges where both teaching and residency occur. And, finally, the goal relating to rental rates may be specified as an objective to provide accommodations at rates ranging from x dollars per academic year to two and one-half times x dollars per year, with the number of residential units at each rate proportional to the variability in economic status among students.

The immediate environmental domain of concern is college housing, but the settings for the housing could be on-campus, adjacent to the campus, or at some distance from the campus, near the center of town. The settings are further defined in terms of space for learning, for intellectual and social functions, and for public and private functions.

Standards and criteria for evaluation of the settings, in this case for evaluation of student housing, are derived from the stated goals and objectives. The primary purpose of the evaluation is to determine if and to what extent the environmental objectives have been met and if the objectives are valid from the vantage point of the user. Standards and criteria define the units of measurement for assessing the quality of the environment. For instance, the objective of campus access is stated directly as fifteen minutes travel time. But the mode of travel is not specified, so the center-of-town setting may meet the criterion as readily as the setting adjacent to the campus, albeit access from the former would be by bus and from the latter by foot. Whether or not both modes of access are equally appealing and satisfying to the students is another important component of the access objective. In other words, there is a qualitative dimension related to the user's expectations, perceptions, and experiences that must also be considered in the evaluation of student housing alternatives. The identification of evaluative standards and criteria must, therefore, lead to measurements that address both the qualitative and the quantitative intent of the goals and objective. In this case, are both forms of access, which are equal in time requirements, equal in terms of student satisfaction?

Definitions

Public policies are statements of normative social values. The idea of goals refers to a desired end-state or ideal expressed, as much as possible, in terms of values inherent in these policies. Objectives define specific actions or attainable conditions intended to further define the stated goal. The goals and objectives delineate relevant environmental settings or domains. Standards and criteria identify the units of comparison or measurement used to substantiate the congruence of accomplishments with goals and objectives. Standards and criteria for some goals and objectives are defined in physical terms and derived by professional or expert judgment from empirical evidence relating to cause-and-effect relationships. For other goals and objectives, however, when such physical terms have not been developed and when cause-and-effect relationships are difficult, if not impossible, to identify in terms of measurable physical attributes, standards and criteria are expressed in more subjective terms relating to the perceptions, experiences, and expectations of users or participants.

Table 1–1 lists selected environmental goals, environmental domains frequently associated with those goals (see Chapter 2), and the primary mode by which standards or criteria are derived. Environmental goals range from the goal of a healthy environment, which frequently encompasses the media of air, water, and sound, and for which measurement standards and criteria are derived from empirical data by professional judgment, to the goal of environmental satisfaction, which encompasses such domains as house, neighborhood, school, and recreation area and for which user experiences and perceptions provide the basis of measurement. Standards and criteria relative to the goals of safety, productivity, and natural process include building codes for structures, fertility for soils, gallons per minute for water supply, biomass and diversity for plant communities, and frequency or density counts for animal communities. Qualitative thresholds are usually derived by professional or expert judgments based on empirical data. Standards and criteria for esthetic environmental domains, however, embrace a mixture of professional judgments and participant-observer judgments. This is probably attributable to a more widely shared experience of landscape, townscape, historical considerations, and recreational needs among nonexperts and, hence, an experiential competence in making such judgments

Table 1–1. Environmental Quality Goals, Related Domains, and Derivation of Standards

Goals	Related Domains	Derivation of Standards
Health	Air, water, sound	Professional judgments
Safety	Structures, transportation systems, flood plains, earthquake zones, earthslide areas	Professional judgments
Productivity	Agricultural areas, forests, wildlife habitats, water	Professional judgments
Natural process	Drainage system, aquifer and recharge zone, plant and animal communities	Professional judgments
Accessibility	Recreation area open space, school, work place	Professional judgments User perceptions and experiences
Aesthetics	Landscape, coastal zone, townscape, historic buildings and places, outdoor recreation, eyesores	Professional judgments User perceptions and experiences
Satisfaction	House, neighborhood, community, work place, school, recreation	User perceptions and experiences

that is not shared in reference to other more technically defined goals. In a very real sense, these domains and media make up the everyday environments of most people.

Standards and criteria, or quality level thresholds, also change over time as new information becomes available that influences professional judgments and user-perceptions and experiences. These standards can also be the subject of considerable disagreement, even among professionals.

One of the most prominent examples of disagreement among professionals has been in the setting of air quality standards for cities in the United States. The air is an important physical domain for the goal of achieving or preserving a healthy environment. There is ample evidence of the relationship of air quality to respiratory diseases in humans, the stunting of plant growth, and the deterioration of structures (Greenwood & Edwards, 1973, p. 149–151). The quality of the air is determined by comparison with standards that are defined as threshold levels of pollutants such as sulfur dioxides, nitrogen dioxide, carbon monoxide, particulate matter, and hydrocarbons. Threshold levels of these measurable elements are established by professional judgment based on available empirical data (Babcock & Nagda, 1972, p. 185), but the disparity among professional opinions, in many cases, has been broad.

Housing, for example, is an important physical domain for the goal of environmental satisfaction. In assessing housing satisfaction there is considerable evidence that, in addition to the actual physical environment, residents' assessments derive from individual aspirations, past residential experiences, and judgments of the relative quality of housing of neighbors, friends, and relatives (Campbell, Converse & Rodgers, 1976). While there is opportunity to invoke objective standards such as number and size of rooms, size of yard or outdoor space, and geographic location, there is also the highly subjective perceptual-experiential component that must be considered in evaluation.

SUBJECTIVITY AND OBJECTIVITY

As indicated by the previous simplified examples and by Table 1–1, environments are evaluated using both objective and subjective measures. The emphasis in this book is on the latter, on using the human perceptual system as a measuring instrument. It is misleading and erroneous, however, to assume that subjectivity and objectivity are mutually exclusive concepts when applied to environmental evaluations. Objective measures are not derived without subjective judgments. The decision as to which characteristics of an environment shall be qualitatively defined with criteria and standards is frequently a subjective decision. Those selected may not necessarily be the most important characteristics, but, rather, the ones for which there are known measurement techniques. In some instances, the most important characteristics may still be unknown.

The complexity of many environmental quality issues has become increasingly obvious, and is manifest in a realization of our lack of knowledge about the cumulative effects and synergistic effects on people of many substances and conditions. Each year brings new knowledge of heretofore unexpected impacts of synthetic compounds on land, air, water, and human health. An additional element of subjectivity enters in with the setting of quality level thresholds for the various domain attributes. In many cases, the empirical data provide for considerable latitude in the setting of thresholds.

In another instance, standards that range from 50 to 3,000 bacteria per 100 milliliters have been adopted in different localities for water used for the same kinds of recreational purposes (Kneese & Bower, 1968, p. 31)—a very wide range indeed.

In social science data, objectivity cannot necessarily be equated with accuracy. Campbell, Converse, and Rogers (1976, p. 475), in discussing objective (unemployment rates, crime rates, number of dwelling units) and subjective (level of expressed satisfaction) social indicators, suggest that the common presumption that measurement error is a far more serious problem for subjective measures, or so-called "soft" data, than for objective measures, or so-called "hard" data, while true in general, can lead to "wild exaggerations." They point to the ambiguity that can exist in the simple counting of empirical cases to determine whether given cases "should or should not be taken as instances of the phenomenon being measured." For example, how is a dwelling unit or a visitor day at a recreation area defined?

The gist of this discussion is that the concern for objectivity is equally applicable to the evaluation of all goals and classes of data, both so-called "hard" data and "soft" data. Measurement systems have to be reliable. The same data should be obtained in repeated applications of the procedures. The measurement system should yield valid measures—that is, it should measure what it purports to measure, and should show changes that occur in the characteristic being measured. And, finally, the measurement should have utility—it should be useful for the promulgation and implementation of policy and the attendant decisions relating to environmental management and modification.

AN EVALUATION SCHEMA

What are the basic elements of evaluation studies?

Thus far it has been suggested that evaluation studies are usually undertaken to assess the adequacy of existing environments and to provide guidance for the creation of new environments or renovation of existing environments. The findings from such studies can, therefore, help in shaping public policies that, in turn, influence the shape of our environment.

The standards and criteria used in evaluation are based on specific goals and objectives derived from public policies—policies usually intended to address societal values, needs, and problems. The standards and criteria cannot be generalized across environmental domains or settings, however, but must be developed, along with appropriate measurements, for specific settings.

Another group of elements central to the kind of evaluation studies being discussed encompasses the users of these environments. The users are the measuring instruments for identifying the quality of different environments. Their past experiences, perceptions, and expectations for the future all enter into the evaluation activity.

Figure 1-2 depicts an evaluation schema that groups these and other elements of evaluation studies into three primary dimensions: institutional, environmental, and participatory. These dimensions provide a useful framework for the design and review of evaluation studies based on the user as a measuring instrument.

The institutional dimension considers why, how, and for whom the study is being done. These are not independent attributes of one dimension, but interact both within the institutional dimension and among all three dimensions. The choice of strategy or, in other words, how the study is to be done, is obviously

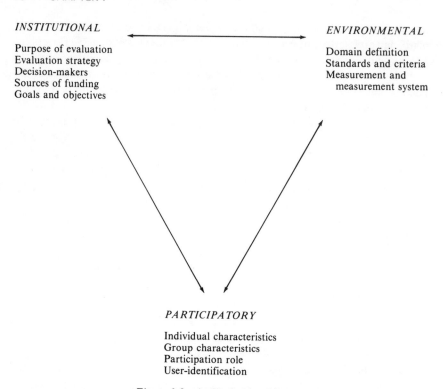

INSTITUTIONAL

Purpose of evaluation
Evaluation strategy
Decision-makers
Sources of funding
Goals and objectives

ENVIRONMENTAL

Domain definition
Standards and criteria
Measurement and
    measurement system

PARTICIPATORY

Individual characteristics
Group characteristics
Participation role
User-identification

Figure 1-2. An Evaluation Schema.

defined by why and for whom (for example, policy maker, administrator, planner, or designer) it is being done and by the goals and objectives. The form of the data should be determined by its intended use if it is to have utility as well as validity and reliability. The strategy will also be determined by the environment being evaluated—whether it is an existing environment or a plan for a future environment—and by such individual or group characteristics of the users as age and education. For example, some strategies might require greater knowledge or more special skills on the part of users and would thus be biased in favor of those with more education.

The environmental dimension encompasses domain definition, physical attributes, standards and criteria, and the measurement system. Domains have been categorized and defined in numerous ways, as indicated in Table 1–1. For example, there are resource definitions such as air, forests, habitats, and water; environmental process definitions such as flood plains, earthquake zones, and aquifer recharge areas; land use or functional definitions such as transportation systems, agriculture, work place, and recreation area; and place-scale definitions such as house, neighborhood, town, city, and region. There is obviously no universal taxonomy that can be superimposed on such widely differing organizational concepts. There are, however, several guidelines that can enhance the utility and efficacy of environmental definitions for evaluation studies:

1. The taxonomy should be policy relevant; the environmental domains relate directly and explicitly to goals and objectives set forth in public policy.
2. The environmental domains should be defined in qualitative terms using standards and criteria or physical dimensions (measurable physical elements, or characteristics) that are sensitive to changes in the domain and that are correlates of the users' or participant-observers' perceptions of quality.
3. The domains should be relevant, not only in terms of physical definitions but also in terms of the perceptual/cognitive processes of participant-observers and decision-makers. The domains must be meaningful to those doing the evaluation and to those for whom it is being done.

The first is a utility criterion. It should be obvious that if evaluation data are to provide feedback information to improve the quality of decision-making with reference to environmental change and modification, there must be explicit semantic and conceptual relationships with the relevant goals and objectives. This criterion also speaks to the need for standard definitions and procedures that allow for comparisons of data and findings from different studies about the same kinds of domains in different places, at different times, or with different users.

The second is a validity and efficacy criterion. The domain should be defined in terms of both salient measurable elements or attributes and relationships between these elements and perceived quality. In other words, it is important to determine whether physical differences among elements are related to measurable changes in the perceived quality of the environment. The significance of these relationships should not be underestimated. The standards and criteria or the physical elements used to define the specific domain and to determine the measurement system ought to reflect both physical differences or changes in the environment and differences in perceptions of quality if the resulting data are to be effective in future decision-making.

Table 1-2 indicates the kinds of elements or characteristics that have been used in several recent studies to define the goals, domains, and associated standards and criteria of the scenic quality of the coastal zone and the liveability of city streets. The coastal zone list is made up of individual or composite physical shoreline characteristics. These characteristics can be manipulated in varying degrees, through management practices or land-planning recommendations, to create varying scenic consequences in the coastal zone. The correlation of these elements or coastal characteristics with users' perceptions of scenic beauty is an indication of their validity. The elements of city street satisfaction are a combination of physical elements (for example, traffic volume and noise) and perceptual/experiential characteristics (for example, privacy and environmental awareness). City residents' perceptions of noise, traffic hazards, and pollution, and self-reports of behaviors such as neighboring and visiting, provide a composite

Table 1–2. Environmental Attributes and Characteristics

Coastal Aesthetics[1]	City Street Satisfaction[2]
Developed shoreline	Traffic volume
Steep rocky shoreline	Traffic hazard
Low-relief shoreline	Stress, noise, and pollution
Salt ponds	Neighboring and visiting
Beaches	Privacy and home territory
Mangrove stands	Environmental awareness

[1] From *Public Attitude Survey, Technical Supplement No. 2*, Virgin Islands Planning Office. Charlotte Amalie, St. Thomas: 1977a (also see Chapter 5).
[2] From *Liveable Urban Streets: Managing Auto Traffic in Neighborhoods*, by D. Appleyard. Washington, D.C., U.S. Government Printing Office, 1976 (also see Chapter 5).

view of perceptions of liveability on different streets in association with different levels of traffic volume. The studies from which these two sets of elements and characteristics are taken are discussed in some detail in Chapter 5.

The third guideline is an efficacy and communications criterion. It assumes that the evaluation of plans, designs, management strategies, and existing environments will be more efficacious if the environment is defined and described in ways relating to users' conceptualizations of the environment. Scientific/technological taxonomies, which are frequently employed by government agencies and professional consultants, can hinder communication among participant-observer subgroups.

Planning reports and documents frequently adopt the classification systems of geologists, ecologists, and land-use specialists and use terms such as dissected plateau; alluvial fan; antecedent stream; oak savanna; northern hardwoods; desert shrub; humid montane forest; and R-1, R-2, and R-3 residential, institutional, and industrial. There is reason to believe, however, that users conceptualize the environment in terms of potential experiential opportunities (Kaplan, S., 1978) and describe it using simpler terms such as hills, farms, and forests (Palmer & Zube, 1976). This fact suggests that in the classification and description of domains for evaluation studies, every effort should be made to identify and invoke the concepts and vocabulary of the users.

The third dimension of the evaluation schema presented in Figure 1-2 is the participatory dimension, which includes the identification of users, individual and group characteristics, and the role of the user or participant.

The concept of the person as a measuring system for environmental evaluation carries with it a number of important concerns and questions. Among the most important is the question of variability among individual and group characteristics. To what extent do users and groups of users agree or disagree about the quality of environments? A number of other concerns are directly related to this question. For example: what background factors, such as childhood experiences, influence perceptions of environmental quality; what is the influence on perception of social institutions such as news media and advertising; and what is the effect on perception of social context such as political system or population homogeneity, and environmental context such as proximity to the environment being evaluated?

In a broad state-of-the-art review of research on perception of environmental quality, Craik and Zube suggest three related attributes as a potential means of focusing on the participatory dimension in terms significant to decision-makers (1976, p. 18). First is the focus of the evaluation as either place-centered or person-centered. A place-centered evaluation addresses an array of places or a set of alternative plans, designs, or management strategies for a single place as the primary unit of analysis, and a person-centered evaluation focuses on a sample of persons. A place-centered evaluation is primarily concerned with the composite or average response of users for comparisons among a number of places. A person-centered evaluation is primarily concerned with an individual's personal environment.

The second attribute is the psychological or instructional set that defines the role and the frame of reference within which the participant-observer conducts the evaluation, either as a comparative appraisal or as a preferential judgment. The former embodies the notion of judging against some implicit or explicit standard of excellence, while the latter invokes an entirely personal, subjective response to specific environments. Participant-observers might, for example, be instructed to evaluate a group of multifamily housing projects with reference to the standard of an excellent or exemplar project within a specific neighborhood, city, state, or region—that is, to use a specific housing project as a yardstick and to compare all others to it. On the other hand, they might be instructed to express their purely personal preferences with regard to the projects as a place to live, whereby they would consider unique requirements of a personal or family nature in evaluating the group of projects.

The third attribute is variability. Craik and Zube suggest that there is a higher probability of low variability, or of higher consensus, among participant-observers on place-centered comparative appraisals than on person-centered preferential judgments. It is suggested, in other words, that higher agreement will be found among users when they are evaluating environments using a common qualitative standard such as the exemplary housing project than when they are evaluating environments using a totally personal, qualitative standard. The policy implications of this distinction are significant. If there is low variability, the average qualitative rating indicates broad agreement among users and probable support for policy- and decision-making or for endorsement of existing environments. If, however, variability is high, indicating greater disagreement among users, the average qualitative ratings may be misleading and only representative of a few users. Simple attention to the average evaluation of all users would overlook the high and low extremes. While evidence relating to this conceptual distinction between comparative appraisals and preferential judgments is limited, it is supportive. Several studies (Coughlin & Goldstein, 1970; Zube, Pitt, &

Anderson, 1975) have found greater agreement among participants on the comparative evaluation of places for scenic beauty, recreation potential, or residential quality than on the stated preferences of participants about the places for purely personal use.

Identification of individual and group characteristics of participant-observers is important for several reasons. First, it provides a basis for analysis of and potential insights into response variability. Second, it can help identify the appropriate users or participants and provides evidence of the relevance of the participants when evaluation studies relate to environments for specific population subgroups such as the very young, the elderly, low-income persons, or the physically disabled. In such cases, these data can indicate to policy- and decision-makers whether those participating in the evaluation are representative of the target population—those for whom the environment was intended.

Personal and group characteristics that were used in the evaluation studies included in Table 1–2 are listed in Table 1–3. The coastal aesthetics study focused on a very limited set of characteristics. They were, however, important to the testing of long-held assumptions about different perceptions and values among residents of the three islands and about different perceptions and values of native and nonnative West Indians.

The expanded set of user characteristics or background data from the study of city street satisfaction provides a way to define the social class of respondents in terms of their occupation, education, income, and stage in the life cycle as defined by age, marital status, and family size. Michelson (1970) suggests that stage in the life cycle, social class, values, and life style or role emphasis (for example, "swinging singles," solid family person, and so on) are all social-science concepts important to environmental concerns. These concepts facilitate the analysis of user-perception data, emphasizing concern for results meaningful to specific environmental and social policies.

Table 1-3. Personal and Group Characteristics

Coastal Aesthetics[1]	City Street Satisfaction[2]
Education	Age
Length of residence in	Place of residence
Virgin Islands	Occupation
Occupation	Education
Sex	Marital status
	Family size
	Sex
	Ethnic group
	Income
	Ability to drive motor vehicle

[1] From *Public Attitude Survey, Technical Supplement No. 2*, Virgin Islands Planning Office. Charlotte Amalie, St. Thomas: 1977a (see also Chapter 5).
[2] From *Liveable Urban Streets: Managing Auto Traffic in Neighborhoods*, by D. Appleyard. Washington, D.C., U.S. Government Printing Office, 1976 (also see Chapter 5).

SUMMARY

This chapter has introduced the idea of environmental evaluation as an activity in which we all engage, consciously or unconsciously, in making decisions about our everyday life. Additionally, the process of evaluation was related to the concept of values. It was suggested that public policy, within a larger social context, is an important medium for the explication of environmental values. In addition, it was suggested that to effectively evaluate environments resulting from policy decisions, the relevant policy must be explicated in terms of goals and objectives with specified measurable standards and criteria. Environments are evaluated to assess the efficacy of policy, to modify or abandon existing policies, and to indicate the need for additional policies. Environments are also evaluated to assess the adequacy or inadequacy of existing environments and to guide the renovation of deficient environments.

Three dimensions were indicated as important ingredients of evaluation studies—institutional, environmental, and participatory. These are interactive dimensions that provide guidance for the design of evaluation studies and suggest relevant questions to be addressed. The institutional dimension considers why, how, and for whom the evaluation is being done. The environmental dimension includes domain definition, physical attributes, criteria, and the measurement system. The participatory dimension includes identification of the characteristics of the users of the environment, and the role of the users in an evaluation study.

CHAPTER EXERCISE

An important thesis of this book, both explicitly and implicitly, is that we should learn from the environment and from the people who use it. We need to know what is valued by the users of the environment, what satisfies their wants and needs, and what fails to satisfy their wants and needs. By studying selected environments and users in a systematic way we can provide policy- and decision-makers with important information about the perceived quality of different environmental domains and milieus.

The purpose of the exercise that follows is to stimulate students to do more than read and talk about evaluation and to start designing and initiating evaluation studies—that is, to learn by doing. Design students should start thinking about evaluation in relation to every building, landscape, or interior design problem they are assigned. Behavioral science students should explore the most effective ways in which their essential contribution can be integrated into the design process—as members of design teams working on programs and on all the succeeding steps, as consultants to designers on selected issues, or as agents, independent of designers, representing the client, users, or sponsoring agency. How best can designers and behavioral scientists participate in environmental evaluation and contribute to the development of the important information profiles needed by policy- and decision-makers? How can they improve their own abilities to design environments that are responsive to and supportive of users' wants, needs, and values?

Prepare a list of environmental attributes and user characteristics for a community housing inventory. As a minimum, consider the following social groups:

young single people
young couples without children
couples with children
elderly couples
single elderly people

What personal and group characteristics are important for such a housing evaluation study? What physical characteristics would you consider? Explain in writing the reasons for each characteristic you have identified. If the class consists of both design students and behavioral science students, single-discipline and multiple-discipline teams should be formed with each team working independently of the others. Comparisons among the team reports should provide insights about the particular orientations and contributions of the different disciplines.

SUPPLEMENTARY READINGS

The following readings are recommended for those who wish to explore in greater depth some of the environmental and behavioral interests and issues central to the concerns of this book. Berry and Horton provide an introduction to perceptual and technical environmental quality issues and to government programs associated with planning and managing a quality environment. Heimstra and McFarling provide an introduction to the broad array of interests and concerns associated with the study of environment and behavior.

Berry, B. J., & Horton, F. E. *Urban environmental management*. Englewood Cliffs, N.J.: Prentice-Hall, 1974.
Heimstra, N. W., & McFarling, L. H. *Environmental psychology*. Monterey, Calif.: Brooks/Cole, 1978.

Chapter 2

SETTING POLICY

THE MEANINGS OF POLICY

The definition of public policy as an expression of public values was introduced in Chapter 1. It was suggested that policy establishes the framework within which programs and projects are developed. Furthermore, it was suggested that policies, which tend to be generalized statements, need to be expressed in more specific terms as goals and objectives in order to facilitate policy implementation in programs and projects. Specific goals and objectives also provide the bench mark or reference point for evaluating the resulting programs and projects and for assessing policy effectiveness. The purpose of this chapter is to provide an overview of the changing patterns of American environmental policy and of the implications of these changes for user-based evaluations.

O'Riordan defines policy as "the mechanism through which society's collective demands are monitored by the political system for conversion into action" (O'Riordan, 1976, p. 55). Simon introduces a further refinement into the definition —that policy involves ethical questions. He argues that "Democratic institutions find their principal justification as a procedure for the validation of value judgments." In theory, the legislative arm of decision-making, be it local, state, or national, is generally held responsible for making the value judgments related to ethical questions. The administrative arm is theoretically responsible for relating those decisions to factual elements. In actual practice, however, the distinction is not always that clear. As Simon points out (1957), many value judgments involve factual questions. The enactment of the National Environmental Policy Act of 1969, which set forth a broad statement of national values, was not based solely on ethical questions and value judgments. There was a considerable body of factual information presented to Congress, in support of the legislation, about trends in the quality of the environment. In addition, value judgments are frequently inherent in the decisions of administrators as they define and select operational objectives to implement legislatively promulgated policy. Given this interplay of factual and ethical or value-oriented decision-making, evaluation is important to both the legislative body and the administrative agency. The legislative body must have access to factual information and advice that will influence and shape future policy as well as modify existing policy. The administrative agency must be responsive to the broad array of community, state, or national values that interact with but are frequently more encompassing than those that are explicitly enacted into law.

The term *policy* is often used in a much broader context than that discussed above. The term is often used to include both policies usually promulgated by legislative bodies to deal with value-oriented ethical questions and those promulgated by management to deal with the rules, regulations, and procedures by which social organizations operate (Simon, 1957). Primary emphasis in this book is on legislative policies—that is, on those dealing with value-oriented, ethical questions.

THE MAKING OF POLICY

The major emphasis of the following overview is on the past one hundred years or so—from the 1860s to the present. Before launching into this discussion, however, it is important to recognize the telescoping effect of such an abbreviated review and to note the intellectual and political climate within which much policy is created. One hundred years, the approximate time span covered in the following policy discussion, is a reasonably long time when viewed in the perspective of contemporary political systems. During this period of time the world has witnessed profound changes in national boundaries and in the creation of new nations. While the changes in the United States' environmental policy noted in the following pages may not seem quite as profound as those in the global political system, they do seem to reflect a profound, if not radical, shift in American values. This shift has, however, been an incremental one, spread out over more than one hundred years. Policy-making is in general an incremental process with small changes made at more frequent intervals rather than widely spaced major changes (Lindblom, 1968). A quick glance at the housing legislation listed in Table 2-1 illustrates this point. The five Acts spanning the time period of 1934 to 1970 are just a sampling of the housing legislation enacted during that time period. The Acts listed in the table, however, generally represent those concepts and legislative efforts by which a number of incremental concepts and changes were synthesized so as to provide new program and project direction.

How does legislative policy come into being? One of three conditions is often associated with policy enactment: crisis, consensus, or indifference. While we are very much aware that extreme geophysical events such as floods, hurricanes, droughts, and earthquakes have an equal probability of occurring every year, policy-makers are much more likely to consider flood management or earthquake-monitoring legislation immediately after an extreme event than in the years between events. The impact of the event frequently dramatizes the inadequacy of existing policy to effectively deal with a very real social and environmental crisis, thus precipitating a kind of knee-jerk reaction among policy-makers.

A favorable climate for the creation of legislative policy also exists when there is consensus among legislators. If the issue at hand is one about which the majority of the legislators agree, policy can be enacted without fear of dissatisfaction among political constituencies.

A climate of indifference supports the creation of policy favorable to special interests. A majority of the legislators may be indifferent to proposed legislation because it addresses a specific project—for example, a park or a highway—that has little or no national significance. The project may be unique to a single state and serve the special needs of a specific sector of one legislator's constituency. The legislation is approved not because it is viewed as good but rather because there is indifference to it.

One final condition merits mention. It concerns the issue of policy implementation, rather than policy creation. After policy is created, funding must follow if it is to be implemented. The new community program of the Housing and Urban Development Act of 1970, for instance, was effectively terminated when funding was severely curtailed in the mid 1970s, even though the policy remained in spirit. The Highway Beautification Act of 1965 is another example. The Act was passed and policy established with regard to roadside eyesores such as junkyards and billboards, but a number of years passed before the Act received funding adequate for implementation of important sections of the legislation. The lesson is that policy at any level of government, in the absence of adequate funds for implementation, represents unfulfilled aspirations and promises.

HISTORICAL PERSPECTIVE

Over the past century, public environmental policy has evolved from a primary focus on land disposal that encouraged development and resource exploitation to a more comprehensive outlook advanced under the rubric of environmental quality. Between these foci, however, policy has embraced the concepts of conservation and reservation, housing and health, and recreation and aesthetics (see Figure 2-1). This chapter is organized around some of the important Federal legislative bench marks that encompass and explicate these several stages. The intent is to review the evolution of national legislative environmental policy in the United States from an historical perspective, to identify important shifts in policy orientation, and to assess the current potential for user-based environmental evaluation.

Disposal and Exploitation

The earliest stage in this evolution of policy is exemplified by the disposal of public lands. The policy of disposal was stimulated because the country was land-rich and money-poor in the early years of its existence. Furthermore, the

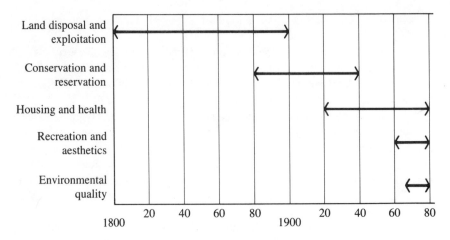

Figure 2-1. Environmental policy foci.

country was confronted with the repayment of debts incurred in the Revolutionary War. Land sales in the late eighteenth and early nineteenth centuries provided one way of raising the necessary funds. Lands were also granted by the federal government to states (225 million acres) and railroads (91 million acres) as a stimulus for development. The granting of alternate sections (640 acres, or one square mile) on each side of a proposed railroad right-of-way in order to subsidize construction and expansion was not uncommon. Under the Morrill Act of 1862, states were granted tracts of land that they, in turn, could sell to finance the development of agricultural colleges ("land-grant" colleges and universities). Over thirteen million acres were given to the states under this program.

Mining laws of the 1860s and 1870s, in particular the Mining Law of 1872, which is still on the books, provided for the conveyance of the surface area of the land as well as the mineral rights under the surface. While this provision was changed in the 1920s, the country is still confronted with privately held mineral rights, acquired during those earlier years, in the midst of publicly owned park and forest lands. A perception of unlimited lands, soils, forests, and minerals, and an apparent lack of concern for their depletion and for the impact of their exploitation on the environment exemplifies this period and was dramatized by mineral exploitation. The adoption of environmentally destructive extractive techniques for certain minerals and the total lack of attention to the rehabilitation of surface-mined areas are problems that persist into the last quarter of the twentieth century.

Among the most important policies relating to land disposal were undoubtedly those set forth in the homestead laws, starting with the Homestead Act of 1862. Two-hundred eighty-five million acres of public land have been disposed of via the various homestead laws enacted and, by 1880, over 1,700,000 farms were created in the plains and western states, many as a result of the homestead laws. Most of these were single-family farms.

Conservation and Reservation

In the latter years of the nineteenth century changing attitudes began to emerge toward the environment and toward land management in particular. These changing attitudes, which were sometimes conflicting, are collectively associated with the conservation movement and were dramatized under the presidency of Teddy Roosevelt. Caldwell (1970, p. 38) points out that the goals and objectives of the conservation advocates did not present a unified front nor lead to a consistent environmental policy. He suggests:

> Some wished to maximize the economic utilization of the environment and were primarily opposed to waste or "non-use" of natural resources; others sought protection of aesthetic value in landscape, waters, and wildlife; a third group saw the natural world as a great laboratory of science and tried to prevent its impoverishment through the indiscriminate destruction of living species and of natural habitats.

These diverse views, with their conflicting values and objectives, led to two distinct perceptions of the conservation mission. One perception was that of utilitarian management and the application of science to ensure sustained economic production—for example, from forests, irrigation of desert lands, and the harnessing of water power. The second perception was that of environmental preservation. This view of the conservation mission, while accepting limited amounts of environmental change, embraced the setting aside or preserving of lands in their natural state to protect them from all development because of their scientific or aesthetic values.

The conservation movement saw the establishment of forest reserves (now called National Forests) under the Forest Reserve Act of 1891, and the creation of National Parks, starting with Yellowstone in 1872. Forest reserves were managed, after passage of the Forest Management Act of 1897, for timber production and protection of water resources. National Park lands, on the other hand, were directed to be preserved. Thus, the two conflicting objectives of the conservation movement were represented initially by lands that were to be the responsibility of the Forest Service and the National Park Service respectively. So-called economic use versus preservation conflicts are still very much a part of environmental management decisions. Different perceptions of rivers, as places for dams or as places for white-water canoeing, and of remote mountain lands, as places for timber harvest or for wilderness recreation, are still very much a part of the policy maker's and resource manager's arena of decision/dilemma.

The policy of reserving lands for various purposes also extended to state governments, as was manifest by the setting aside of state forests, parks, wetlands, wildlife reserves, and current efforts (in some states) to reserve the most productive agricultural lands. However, while many of the policies and practices associated with the conservation movement still exist today, the major thrust, the formative years, and the sharpening of the issues occurred mainly between 1880 and 1930.

Caldwell (1970) summarizes the conservation movement as the first organized protest by the American people against the degradation of the national environment. The initial concern was as much with economic waste as with abuses of nature. He argues further that by the mid-twentieth century the fears of depleted or disappearing resources had been allayed by prominent resource economists and that with this de-emphasizing of alarmist proclamations about the nation running out of critical raw materials, the weight of the conservationists' arguments shifted to aesthetic and ecological considerations.

Housing and Health

Many popular treatises on the environment contribute to an erroneous or, at best, incomplete image of environmental issues as encompassing only "nature" and "natural elements" such as air, water, and forests. As such they ignore the fact that the important environment for most people is urban, important because the majority of Americans live in settings best described as urban or suburban. Within these settings the quantity and quality of housing has been a public policy issue since the 1930s. The health of the environment, as indicated by the quality of water and air, has been recognized at least since the mid-nineteenth century. The air-polluting effects of the industrial revolution and the association of typhoid epidemics with water pollution gave reasons for alarm and, at the local or municipal level, stimulated a number of successful efforts, by the start of the twentieth century, to provide safe drinking water. It was not until the late 1940s and 1950s, however, that comprehensive policies and programs were launched at the federal level. Noise, another atmospheric condition associated with health, was not recognized in Federal legislation until 1968.

Initial impetus for housing policy, associated with the 1930s depression, was mixed. The National Housing Act of 1934 was intended as both a stimulus to the economy, to resuscitate a stagnant building industry, and as a means of providing low-income housing in healthful surroundings. The United States Housing Act of 1937, also designed to combat the depression, was intended to not only provide housing for the poor but also to clear slums from American cities. This Act marked the beginning of public housing—that is, subsidized housing for the poor. It also redefined the term *slum* to include the physical environment—the condition of buildings, the absence of amenities, and the density of development.

The Housing Act of 1949 extended Federal concern with slum clearance and proposed a national program of urban renewal that promised a suitable living environment for every American family. The Housing Act of 1954 was intended to redirect the Federal slum-clearance and renewal program, which had not achieved the momentum envisioned in the 1949 Act, and to prevent the spread of slums, which had occurred at a greater rate than slum clearance since 1949, by rehabilitating and improving vulnerable areas. The 1954 Act also provided financial assistance to states and local units of government for comprehensive city planning that in most instances, focused on the physical environment.

The Interstate Highway and Defense Act of 1956 not only launched the planning and construction of the Interstate Highway System, but also precipitated major change in city environments through improvements in urban highways. New highways were frequently routed through areas offering the least resistance, such as slums, or through park lands where land acquisition costs were minimal and middle- and upper-income neighborhoods could be avoided.

Abrams (1965) has criticized most housing policies as lacking realistic environmental objectives relating to the difficult problems of population distribution and location. Federal programs have accelerated the move of middle-class residents to suburbia but have only allowed for the redistribution of slum dwellers from one slum to another within the boundaries of the cities. Abrams argues that the city has not been made a more attractive place to live for middle-class Americans and the suburb has not been made accessible to the poor family. Housing policy has also tended to foster a continued emphasis on the owner-occupied, single-family detached dwelling on its individual plot of land. Public housing policy has only provided a modest stock of dwelling units and some of these have been severely criticized for failure to support the specific needs, life-styles, or stages in the life-cycle of the intended residents.

The Housing and Urban Development Act of 1970 provided a short-lived program of financial assistance to private developers and state development agencies for new communities. The goals or objectives of the new towns or new communities, as stated in the Act, encompassed concerns for population migration, preservation of desirable aspects of natural environments, economic feasibility, comprehensive physical and social planning, community infrastructure, provision of low- and moderate-income housing, and the use of advanced design concepts and construction technologies. The new towns were envisioned as demonstration laboratories responding, at least in part, to the criticisms of earlier housing and urban policies. Thirteen new town projects were initiated and given financial support under this program. The declining economy and serious recession of the mid-1970s worked against the experiment before it got off to a reasonable start. By 1978 the Secretary of the Department of Housing and Urban Development acknowledged the failure of the program and initiated steps to end the new effort.

Although the initial concern with air quality stemmed from the prevalence of industrial smoke and was manifest by the passage of smoke-control laws in Chicago and Cincinnati as early as 1881, the complexity of the apparently increasing problem wasn't realized until the principal sources of photochemical smog were identified as hydrocarbons and nitrogen-oxides from automobile exhausts. Air pollution was no longer confined solely to heavily industrialized cities but could also constitute a problem of major dimensions in a city such as Los Angeles, which is dependent on the private automobile as a primary means of transportation.

The first action-oriented federal legislation was the Clean Air Act of 1963, which provided grants to states and municipal air-pollution agencies and began to address regional and inter-state pollution problems. The Act was amended in 1965 to permit national regulation of the emission of pollutants from new cars. The Comprehensive Air Quality Act of 1967 set forth a new approach to the regional problem and called for the designation of air quality regions, the promulgation of standards relating to the harmful effects of pollutants on health, vegetation, and materials, definition of control technologies, and plans and time-tables for implementing the standards by source of pollutant. Under the Clean Air Amendment of 1970 the Environmental Protection Agency was charged with the responsibility for setting air quality standards for the entire nation. The Act also called for states to develop implementation plans for the standards.

Berry and Horton (1974, p. 199) indicate that around 1875 the spread of disease in cities and a beginning knowledge of microbiology brought increased attention to the public treatment of sewage. This attention, however, was primarily at the municipal or local level. The increasing magnitude of the water pollution problem and the interstate or regional effects of upstream communities dumping their wastes into rivers and streams used as sources of municipal water by downstream communities eventually stimulated federal involvement. The Federal Water Pollution Control Act of 1956 authorized grants to states for planning and technical assistance and for the construction of municipal water treatment plants. The Act was amended in 1965 to include the establishment of water quality standards and called for the cleanup of all interstate and coastal waters. In 1972, the passage of further amendments established two general goals (Berry & Horton, 1974, p. 201):

1. To achieve, wherever possible, by July 1, 1983, water that is clean enough for swimming and other recreational uses, and clean enough for the propagation of fish, shellfish, and wildlife.
2. By 1985, to have no discharges of pollutants into the nation's water.

These amendments set standards and deadlines for the control of pollution from industrial and municipal sources. They also replaced the 1899 Refuse Act with a more stringent permit system, to be administered by the Environmental Protection Agency, for the discharge of pollutants in the nation's waters.

Housing and environmental health policies have evolved over the past thirty to forty years with a gradually broadening perspective. As indicated by the history of housing legislation, however, the policy impetus may be as strongly related to economic goals as to environmental goals. And, regardless of the policy impetus, implementation is tied to the nation's economy. For example, the recession of the 1970s had a dramatic impact on the curtailment of the new communities program of the Housing and Urban Development Act of 1970. Housing policy has tended to support the construction of single-family detached houses rather than a range of alternative housing forms. National policies and programs, as indicated by Abrams (1965), have also lacked specific environmental goals or objectives and have not addressed regional problems of migration and population location. The standards used are those reflected in zoning and building codes at the local or state level.

Air and water quality policies and programs, in contrast to housing, have moved from local or state level standards to the promulgation of standards at the federal level. This trend has undoubtedly been abetted by the recognition of the interstate or regional effects of air and water pollution. The policies and programs are, however, as susceptible to the whims of the economy as housing. The energy crisis has generated arguments for the reduction of air quality standards so as to allow for the burning of lower-cost, higher-sulfur-content fossil fuels and for the postponement of the timetable for the implementation of certain standards.

Recreation and Aesthetics

Recreation and aesthetics were certainly policy issues during the heyday of the conservation movement, and were in part embedded in the philosophy supporting the establishment of some of the earliest reservations. The Act creating the National Park Service in 1916 stated:

> The service thus established shall promote and regulate the use of Federal areas known as national parks, monuments, and reservations hereinafter specified by such means and measures to conform to the fundamental purpose of said parks, monuments, and reservations, which purpose is to conserve the scenery and the natural and historic objects and the wildlife therein, and to provide for the enjoyment of the same in such manner and by such means as will leave them unimpaired for the enjoyment of future generations.

This Act established for all parks, as a matter of policy, the guiding management principles first set down with the establishment of Yellowstone National Park. It also includes explicit reference to recreation as "enjoyment," and to aesthetics in the mandate to "conserve the scenery."

Forest service lands were used for recreation purposes at an increasing rate in the 1920s and 1930s, but the major increase, if not explosion, in outdoor recreation on forest and park lands occurred after World War II. The Multiple-Use Sustained Yield Act of 1960 gave the Forest Service statutory authority to manage lands for recreation as well as for timber production and watershed protection, a responsibility it had not previously held. This Act also imposed a responsibility to manage for aesthetics, as scenic quality was frequently associated with the quality of the recreation experience.

The 1965 Wilderness Act addressed a special kind of recreational and aesthetic value, as well as scientific and ecological values. The Wilderness Act set aside some 9.1 million acres of forest lands and called for a ten-year review of other forest and park land and wildlife refuges for their potential inclusion in the wilderness system. It represented a victory for the kind of conservation program advocated by the preservationists earlier in the twentieth century. By 1976 an additional 5.3 million acres had been added to the system and proposals had been developed to add approximately 25 million acres more (including 19.2 million acres in Alaska).

The Land and Water Conservation Fund Act of 1965 authorized federal agencies to acquire land for recreation purposes and provided funds for federal, state, and local purchase of lands. The Act established a fund with an annual income of 200 million dollars through 1970 and 300 million dollars thereafter through June of 1989. It provided for land acquisition in both urban and nonurban areas.

Additional legislation during the 1960s led to the adoption of the National Trails System Act of 1968 and the National Wild and Scenic Rivers Act of 1968. Both of these Acts were addressed to the management of specific sectors of the environment because of their particular scenic and recreational values. By 1977, 116 trails extending over 1000 miles in length were designated as National Recreation Trails. In addition, two trails were designated as National Scenic Trails and 14 others were put under study. Some 78 rivers or parts thereof were originally proposed for inclusion in the Rivers System. As of 1977, 19 rivers were in the system, 60 more were either under study or had been proposed for inclusion and were awaiting the action of Congress, and portions of 20 others had been proposed for study. Almost 50% of the states have also adopted state-level wild-and-scenic-river programs to augment the national effort.

Aesthetic environmental concerns during the 1960s extended beyond recreation, wilderness, and natural areas to encompass highway roadsides, the appearance of cities and towns, and the impacts of strip mining. The focal point of these concerns was the White House Conference on Natural Beauty called by President Johnson in 1965. The conference provided a forum for a broad discussion of environmental ills throughout the nation and was, in many respects, a forerunner of the "environmental quality" movement that followed. In his message to Congress on February 8, 1965 President Johnson stated:

> We must not only protect the countryside and save it from destruction, we must restore what has been destroyed and salvage the beauty and charm of our cities. Our conservation must be not just the classic conservation of protection and development, but a creative conservation of restoration and innovation. Its concern is not with nature alone, but with the total relationship between man and the world around him. Its object is not just man's welfare, but the dignity of man's spirit.

In this message, the President declared his support of the then proposed programs for scenic rivers, trails, and highways and also ennumerated a long list of environmental ills subsequently discussed at the White House Conference held on May 24 and 25. Following this national conference, about half the states conducted follow-up meetings addressing problems and opportunities at the political and geographical scale of the individual states.

The momentum initiated by these activities was never realized, nor was the actual commitment of the Johnson administration to environmental issues ever tested. Increasing national concern with the growing involvement in Viet Nam, coupled with unrest and riots in the cities and on university campuses, directed attention away from environmental issues and natural beauty to a set of pressing social problems.

Environmental Quality

Caldwell (1970, p. 62) suggests "It was an intuitive sensing of widespread popular desire, and not the counsel and endorsement of important people nor the pressure of political activists, which moved the Ninety-first Congress to bipartisan adoption of the National Environmental Policy Act of 1969." He suggests, in other words, that there was a broad consensus within Congress. He also argues that the earlier natural beauty movement of the 1960s, which, in fact, was the seedbed for the broader concept of environmental quality, represented a "consumer" orientation toward the environment, an orientation made more explicit in the broader concept of environmental quality. Citizen dissatisfaction with and resistance to new highway locations, the loss of parkland, the division and destruction of neighborhoods by highways or urban renewal, housing designs that did not meet users' needs, the draining of wetlands for development, offshore drilling for oil, the location of power-generating facilities in sensitive environmental areas, and the routing of transmission lines through scenic areas or residential neighborhoods prompted demands for citizen involvement in the decision-making process.

The environmental quality concept generated in the 1960s is not only consumer-oriented, but also is comprehensive and long-range in outlook. It is an integrative concept. The National Environmental Policy Act (NEPA) declared that the Federal government has a continuing responsibility

to improve and coordinate Federal plans, functions, programs, and resources to the end that the Nation may—

(1) Fulfill the responsibilities of each generation as trustee of the environment for succeeding generations;
(2) Assure for all Americans safe, healthful, productive, and aesthetically and culturally pleasing surroundings;
(3) Attain the widest range of beneficial uses of the environment without degradation, risk to health or safety, or other undesirable and unintended consequences;
(4) Preserve important historic, cultural, and natural aspects of our national herit-

age and maintain, whenever possible, an environment which supports diversity and variety of individual choice;

(5) Achieve a balance between population and resource use which will permit high
standards of living and a wide sharing of life's amenities; and

(6) Enhance the quality of renewable resources and approach the maximum attainable recycling of depletable resources.

The Act also specified a number of responsibilities for all agencies of the
Federal government including:

1. The use of a systematic, interdisciplinary approach involving natural and social
   sciences and the environmental design arts in decision-making.
2. The identification and development of methods and procedures to ensure that
   environmental amenities and values are given appropriate consideration in decision-making, along with economic and technical considerations.
3. The preparation of a report on the environmental impact of every major Federal
   action significantly affecting the quality of the environment. The report is to
   identify: adverse environmental effects associated with the implementation of
   the proposal; alternatives to the proposed action; the relationship between short-
   term and long-term effects; and irreversible and irretrievable commitments of
   resources should the proposed action be implemented. Copies of the report and
   the comments of appropriate Federal, State, and local agencies are to be made
   available to the public.
4. The study and development of alternatives for any proposed action "which
   involves unresolved conflicts concerning alternative uses of available resources."
5. The recognition of the world-wide and long-range character of environmental
   problems and cooperation in anticipating and preventing decline in the quality of
   the global environment.
6. The provision of advice and information relative to environmental quality
   issues.
7. The utilization of ecological information in project planning and development.

The Coastal Zone Management Act (CZMA) of 1972 exemplifies many of
the environmental quality concerns delineated in the NEPA and attempts to make
them operational relative to a specific sector of the American environment. The
CZMA requires each participating state or territory to include in the management
program, "a definition of what shall constitute permissible land and water uses
within the coastal zone which have a direct and significant impact on coastal
water." It also calls for, "giving full consideration to ecological, cultural, historic, and aesthetic values" as well as to needs for economic development. In other
words, it was the intent of Congress that a broad range of values be considered
and that the long-term impacts of management proposals, as well as short-term
impacts, be considered. Public participation was identified as an essential element of program development.

The implications of the NEPA for environmental evaluation are impressive. It calls for consideration of a broad range of values, systematic approaches,

the development of alternatives, evaluation of short-term and long-term impacts, and for making all information available to the public. It is, in addition, a public disclosure law that provides a basis for citizen intervention in the decision-making process. The requirements for the consideration of alternatives and the analysis of impacts have also affected the planning and design process in most Federal agencies by making it more difficult to only develop that plan or design perceived by the professionals to be "best."

SUMMARY

This brief overview of American environmental policy has focused primarily on federal legislative policy and has left virtually untouched the vast bodies of state and municipal legislative policies dealing with land taxes, zoning, building codes and the like, as well as relevant administrative policies, which frequently specify modes of implementation. It does, however, trace the changing pattern of policy emphasis over the 200 year history of the country (see Figure 2–1) from land disposal and exploitation to a broad concern with the quality of the environment. Important legislative bench marks in this changing pattern are indicated in Table 2–1. Of particular importance to the issue of environmental evaluation is the consumer orientation of policy during the past decade, in particular starting with the National Environmental Policy Act of 1969.

As noted earlier, the change from a dominant policy focus of land disposal and exploitation to one of environmental values and consumer orientation represents a profound, if not radical, change in our public policy. It is important, however, to remember that these changes came gradually and incrementally and, furthermore, that some of the changes might almost be viewed as fortuitous products of a particular point in time.

It took the enactment of the Federal Land Policy and Management Act of 1976 to formally terminate the land disposal policy of the Bureau of Land Management, a policy that was a vestige of the disposal practices of the 1860s. In spite of the passage of the Surface Mining Control and Reclamation Act of 1977, the provisions of the Mining Law of 1872 still prevail for hard-rock mining (deep pits and underground mining) on public lands. While controls are being developed for surface mine operations, hard rock mining on public lands is essentially immune from control for protection of the environment.

The environmental legislation of the 1960s and early 1970s constitutes a body of policy that came into being partly by the fortuitous convergence of several important factors. Certainly one can discern an historically ever-broadening scope to public environmental policy. By the early 1960s, issues of conservation, health, outdoor recreation, and others, had been or were being demonstrated to be politically viable issues at all levels of government. The opportunity for consensus among policy-makers was great. Furthermore, the American economy was, in general, healthy. In the late 1960s, the riots in American cities and the war in Viet Nam, followed in the early 1970s by the

Table 2–1. Public Policy Relating to the Development, Planning, and Management of the Physical Environment: Legislative Bench Marks

1862	Homestead Act	*Authorized a quarter section (160 acres) of the public domain to any citizen or prospective citizen who applied, built a house on the land, farmed a part of it, lived on it for 5 years, and paid a filing fee of $10.00*
1862	Morrill Land Grant College Act	*Granted public lands in the West to states to finance the development of agricultural and mechanical colleges in each state*
1872	Mining Law	*Provided for miners to obtain title to both mineral rights and land surface of public mineral-bearing lands*
1872	Yellowstone Act	*Created the first National Park*
1891	Forest Reserve Act	*Authorized the establishment of forest reserves*
1897	Forest Management Act	*Provided for the management of forest reserves for timber and water flow*
1899	Refuse Act	*Prohibited discharges and deposits into navigable waters without a permit*
1911	Weeks Forest Purchase Act	*Authorized purchase of lands for national forests east of the Mississippi and for purposes of protecting watersheds and stream flow*
1916	National Parks Act	*Created the National Park Service for purposes of managing park lands*
1934	Taylor Grazing Act	*Provided for the management of unreserved public lands for grazing and other purposes*
1934	National Housing Act	*Established the Federal Housing Administration and encouraged home ownership as a matter of policy*
1935	Soil Erosion Act	*Created the Soil Conservation Service and provided for granting of aid to private individuals and public agencies for the control of soil erosion*
1937	United States Housing Act	*Provided for the construction of federally funded public housing*
1945	Federal Water Pollution Control Act	*Authorized grants to states for planning and technical assistance and for municipal waste-treatment plants*

Table 2-1. (continued)

1949	Housing Act	Provided federal assistance for urban renewal involving slum clearance and the promise of a suitable living environment for every American family
1954	Housing Act	Provided financial assistance for state and local comprehensive planning and encouraged rehabilitation as well as redevelopment
1956	Interstate Highway and Defense Act	Provided for the planning and construction of the Interstate Highway System and for improvements in urban highways
1960	Multiple Use and Sustained Yield Act	Provided for multiple-use management of national forests, including timber production, watershed protection, and recreation
1963	Clean Air Act	Provided grants to agencies for pollution control programs
1964	Wilderness Act	Created a wilderness system out of selected lands from national forests, national parks, and wildlife refuges
1965	Land and Water Conservation Fund Act	Authorized federal agencies to acquire land for outdoor recreation and provided grants for federal, state, and local land purchases
1965	Federal Water Pollution Control Act Amendments	Called for establishment of water quality standards and implementation plans for all interstate and coastal waters
1967	Comprehensive Air Quality Act	Provided for a regional approach to establishing and enforcing federal/state air quality standards
1969	National Environmental Policy Act	Established the Council on Environmental Quality, declared a national policy of a quality environment, and called for the assessment of environmental impacts of all major federal actions
1970	Clean Air Act Amendments	Charged the Environmental Protection Agency with responsibility for setting air quality standards for the entire country
1970	Housing and Urban Development Act	Provided financial assistance to private developers and state development agencies for new communities

Table 2-1. (continued)

1972	*Federal Water Control Act Amendments*	*Called for a broad program to prevent, reduce, and eliminate water pollution*
1972	*Noise Control Act*	*Required the Environmental Protection Agency to set noise emission standards for manufactured products and operation of equipment, and to propose controls for aircraft noise and sonic booms*
1972	*Coastal Zone Management Act*	*Provided grants to states and territories for planning and managing the coastal zone with attention to the aesthetic, ecological, and economic values*
1974	*Forest and Rangeland Renewable Resources Planning Act*	*Provided for a comprehensive assessment of renewable resources along with long-range programs for managing public forest resources administered by the U.S. Forest Service*
1976	*Federal Land Policy and Management Act*	*Provided for the official termination of the conveying of Bureau of Land Management lands into private hands and for the multiple use and sustained yield of the Bureau's 473 million acres so as to protect their scientific, scenic, historical, ecological, environmental, air, atmospheric, and water resources, and archaeological values*
1977	*Surface Mining Control and Reclamation Act*	*Established nationwide environmental control over strip mining and required reclamation of the land after mining*

energy crisis and an economic recession, and in the mid and late 1970s by inflation, created a new set of priorities for policy-makers and shifted the emphasis away from the environment. Nevertheless, there was a body of environmental policy that had been created, and public constituencies continued to champion its cause. The consumer orientation that accompanied much of this legislation provided an important mechanism for facilitating the effective participation of these environmental constituencies.

CHAPTER EXERCISES

Select a specific environmental topic such as recreation, conservation, housing, aesthetics, air or water quality, or noise, and investigate the historic development of policy relating to this topic in your community or state. Has the policy changed over time? Can you categorize these changes as reflections of changing social values? If so, how do you interpret and define these changing values?

Select two or more environmental topics and compare current policies at the local and/or state level in reference to consumer orientation. Is there a difference in the consumer orientation between topics or between local and state policies? If so, what is the nature of the difference?

SUPPLEMENTARY READINGS

Two books are suggested for those interested in the historical evolution of environmental policy in America. Caldwell focuses on policy and management issues that led to and supported the concept of environmental quality of the 1960s. The book by Petula presents an encompassing picture of the patterns of use and conservation of our natural resources from the Colonial period to the twentieth century.

Caldwell, L. K. *Environment: A challenge to modern society*. Garden City, N.Y.: The Natural History Press, 1970.
Petula, J. M. *American environmental history*. San Francisco: Boyd & Fraser, 1977.

Chapter 3

THE POLICY/PRACTICE GAP

DEFINING THE GAP

Essentially, every major piece of environmental legislation since the NEPA, as well as some pre-NEPA legislation (see Chapter 4) has called for the involvement of citizens in various review and advisory roles—including the evaluation of management and development proposals. There has also been a growing tendency for both state legislatures and Congress to call for evaluation studies to assist in assessing the effectiveness of existing policy and as an important contribution to the formulation of new policies.

In spite of these efforts, user-based environmental evaluation is still conducted in an uneven and, for some purposes, a seemingly sporadic manner. As indicated in later chapters, citizen contributions to and participation in public decision-making has been institutionalized in a number of environmental programs, but the form of participation is often such that it cannot reasonably be presumed to result in objectively derived, valid evaluations. Obviously, there is a gap between the provisions of legislative policy and the practices of agencies charged with the implementation of those policies.

The reasons for this policy/practice gap are several: decision-makers' perceptions of the validity and reliability of social-science data, inadequate funding to support user-based evaluations, the resistance of agencies to change established practices and procedures, questions about the utility of perceptually based data for decision-making, the state-of-the-art in environmental perception research, and communication problems among the various disciplines and professions involved in the policy formulation-implementation-evaluation continuum. This chapter discusses these reasons for the policy/practice gap, and some of the techniques or strategies being used to close the gap.

DIFFERENCES AMONG PARTICIPANTS
IN THE EVALUATION ACTIVITY

Administrators, decision-makers or professional bureaucrats, physical scientists, social scientists, planners, designers, and the general public (or publics) are all involved in processes relating to environmental planning, design, manage-

34

ment, and evaluation. Decision-makers are responsible for developing and implementing policy, scientists are frequently responsible for conducting evaluation studies, and planners and designers are responsible for producing environmental modification and management proposals for specific programs and projects. Members of the public are called on to review proposals, to participate in the process in numerous other ways, and, finally, to live with the changes that result from implementation. Differences among many of these participants have been noted as contributing to the gap between policy or intention and practice or implementation.

A study by the Institute for Social Research (Caplan et al., 1975) suggests that decision-makers frequently perceive social scientists to be politically naive. This can probably be attributed, in part, to different approaches to problems and problem-solving by decision-makers and scientists. For example, decision-makers have a primary responsibility for the resolution of problems—that is, for instituting the kinds of changes that will bring about a set of conditions perceived to be better in some way than those that previously existed. Scientists, however, are frequently more interested in understanding the nature of the problem than in effecting change. Rachel Kaplan (1973) suggests that planners and designers (and decision-makers) are also more readily accepted by the public as agents of change than are social scientists. Certainly, the kind of information available through public media—radio, TV, and newspapers—about the activities of designers and planners as the creators of buildings, parks, zoning ordinances, and traffic circulation schemes supports this thesis.

Ostrander (1974) proposes that differences in modes of communication may constitute an important difference between designer and scientist. He suggests that the designer's reliance on visual modes of cognizing and communicating and the behavioral scientist's reliance on semantic modes represent two distinct professional cultures and that these differences may create stress when communications are attempted. This argument is also relevant to communications between designers and decision-makers.

Altman (1975) identifies four general differences in the scientist's approach and the designer's approach. He suggests that the typical environmental designer usually studies a particular unit or place such as a home or neighborhood, while the typical behavioral scientist studies a particular phenomenon or social process such as privacy, territoriality, or crowding. A second difference he notes is that of the criterion-orientation of the designer and the process-orientation of the scientist. The designer is oriented to dependent variables —for example, walls, ceilings, and room-size—as they relate to the solution of a specific problem such as the design of an elementary school. The scientist is oriented to the specification and manipulation of independent variables to produce differences in behavioral outcomes—for example, manipulating the arrangement of furniture in a dormitory lounge so as to study the effects of different arrangements on communication among students. A third difference involves the synthesizing nature of the designer's activities and the analyzing nature of many of the scientist's activities. While one is putting things together —for example, designing a house or planning a neighborhood—the other pursues a study of individual variables or specific behaviors—for example, the relationship of age and sex to children's play in supervised playgrounds. The fourth difference Altman suggests is that of the doing and implementing nature of the designer's responsibilities and the knowing and understanding thrust of the scientist's interests. This difference probably exists between decision-makers and scientists also.

Efforts to reduce these differences are noticeable in educational programs in which environmental psychology or sociology courses enroll students from both the planning and design professions as well as the sciences. Such efforts are also reflected in interdisciplinary team approaches employed by some design and planning studio courses. The interdisciplinary team is becoming a more widely used technique in both public and private professional offices as well. For example, the National Park Service organizes, for individual parks, master- or management-planning teams composed of social and physical scientists as well as planners and designers. These efforts work toward a shared understanding of different approaches and different modes of cognizing and communicating.

Obviously, if these differences prevail among decision-makers, scientists, and planning and design professionals, therefore requiring special attention to provide a more efficacious process of policy planning and implementation, they must also prevail among members of the public. Of paramount importance to the development of understanding among all these groups is the issue of communication. Bishop (1976) emphasizes this point when he describes public participation as essentially an information/communication process. The important topic of public participation, including modes of participation and examples of communication efforts with particular relevance to environmental evaluation, will be addressed in the following chapters.

INSTITUTIONAL RESPONSES TO CURRENT POLICY

How do institutions respond to the idea of environmental evaluation and to the use of social-science data in decision-making? In 1970, no state legislature had a full-time staff member involved in program evaluation, but by 1975 over a dozen states had committees, commissions, or auditors' offices functioning in this area, and more such groups were appearing regularly (Chadwin, 1975). What percentage of the effort of these groups is directed to environmental issues is highly conjectural, but it seems reasonable to assume that environmental issues have not been totally ignored as states cope with such problems as housing, recreation, and transportation. Frequently, in the absence of other reliable and valid measures, the measure of program effectiveness has been client- or citizen-satisfaction, thus calling for the use of user surveys.

User surveys are reported to have two attractions for legislative-evaluations. First, legislators, who are the intended audience for these evaluation studies and who must be responsive to their public constituencies, recognize the utility of user surveys "particularly if the objectivity, reliability, and limitations of those surveys are properly explained." And, second, "citizen surveys or user evaluations are, in effect, consumer research in the public sector" (Chadwin, 1975, p. 47). Obviously, this latter attribute is very much in harmony with the consumer orientation of most recent environmental legislation.

A recent study by the Institute of Social Research at the University of Michigan probed the policy/practice gap in greater depth (Caplan et al., 1975). This study investigated the use of and attitudes toward social-science information by 204 federal agency upper-level decision-makers in Washington, D.C.

Based on lengthy interviews (an average of one and one-half hours each) with these decision-makers, the investigators reached a number of conclusions pertinent to our discussion. They found that there is reason for modest satisfaction with the use of social-science information, but they were unable, in the absence of comparative data, to ascertain whether the instances of use were high or low in reference to other kinds of data. Social-science information, which the investigators defined as primarily empirically derived information from psychology, sociology, anthropology, political science, and interdisciplinary fields such as behavioral-economics, behavioral-geography, and psychiatry, was used by a broad array of agencies and for a diverse listing of policy-area decisions. Table 3–1 indicates the policy areas and the percentage of instances of use based on 575 specific reported instances by 185 respondents. Of the policy areas listed in Table 3–1, environment, housing, transportation, recreation, and some issues from the "other" category, such as community development, undoubtedly encompass concern with the physical environment.

The interview data indicated that sociology, psychology, and interdisciplinary areas were the three most frequently cited sources of information. The three research areas reported as providing the most information were program-evaluation, survey research, and demographic research. The three research techniques perceived to be most valid and reliable were (1) observations in real-life situations by trained observers, (2) survey research, and (3) controlled field-experiments. The techniques perceived as least valid and reliable were, in descending order, analysis of archival records, public opinion polling, organizational analysis, and experimental games and simulation. Laboratory experiments and clinical case histories occupied middle positions on the scale of validity and reliability.

Decision-makers tended to use social-science data more for developing an overall view of an issue or to support a decision that had already been made than for specific decisions on specific issues. Furthermore, the research data they used was more often undertaken or commissioned by the agencies than obtained from purely academic research.

The study also inquired into social-indicator data relative to policy formulation and program evaluation. The notion of social indicators encompasses measurement and monitoring of social phenomena associated with the quality of

Table 3-1. Distribution of Social-Science Information Use by Policy Area*

Policy Area	Percentage of Instances of Use
Organizational management	11
Education	8
Health	8
Crime	7
Communications	7
Public opinion management	7
Welfare	7
Military	6
Employment	6
Other	6
Civil rights and minority affairs	5
Environment	4
Housing	4
Transportation	4
International relations	3
Research methodology	3
Consumer affairs	2
Recreation	2
	100

*From *The Use of Social Science Knowledge in Policy Decisions at the National Level,* by N. Caplan, A. Morrison, and R. J. Stambaugh. Copyright 1975 by the University of Michigan. Reprinted by permission of the Institute for Social Science Research, University of Michigan.

life on a national scale (U.S. Department of Commerce, 1977). Social indicators are analogous to such economic indicators as the Gross National Product. Social indicator data were mentioned by 94 percent of the respondents as being of value for their own agencies. Table 3-2 shows the percentage of decision-makers who indicated specific policy areas for which social indicator data were mentioned. At least five of these areas relate to the physical environment, or, to be more explicit, to perceptions of the quality of various environmental domains: housing, environment, demographic (land-use), recreation, and transportation. It seems reasonable to assume that other policy areas such as health and work satisfaction also have some tangible relationships with the quality of the physical environment.

The investigators found the attitudes of the decision-makers toward social science in general had a significant relationship with the use of social-science information. Perceived objectivity of research (that is, reliability and validity), intuitive evaluation of its correctness, and sensitivity to its political implications were found to be the most important attitudinal factors related to information use. Objectivity and political feasibility were adjudged to be probably the most important, with most respondents sharing a belief that social scientists were politically naive and therefore not producing the kind of information needed by decision-makers.

Table 3-2. Distribution of the Mention of Social Measures by Policy Area*

Policy Area	Percentage of Social Measures Mentioned
Health	15
Work satisfaction	13
Attitudes toward government and other primary institutions	13
Education	11
Housing	8
Environment (ecology)	8
Military	7
Demographic (land-use, population growth)	6
Crime	6
Recreation	4
Race relations	4
Drugs	3
Transportation (access & safety)	2
	100

*From *The Use of Social Science Knowledge in Policy Decisions at the National Level,* by N. Caplan, A. Morrison, and R. J. Stambaugh. Copyright 1975 by the University of Michigan. Reprinted by permission of the Institute for Social Science Research, University of Michigan.

The Example of Social Impact Assessment (SIA)

A review of the literature on the contribution of the social sciences to environmental impact assessment, a specific form of program and project evaluation, provides a specific example of the state-of-the-art of social-science information use in decision-making. Two recent volumes (Finsterbusch & Wolf, 1977; Wolf, 1974) include reviews of the social impacts of water resources developments, energy facilities, highways, open space, and flood management, as well as state-of-the-art critiques and discussions about assessment methods. A frequently recurring theme is the absence of a generally accepted definition of social impacts. In some instances, "social" is defined primarily in terms of general community and neighborhood characteristics (Perfater, 1974, p. 109), while in others (Deane & Mumpower, 1977) a more encompassing definition is adopted that includes micro or psychological attributes and characteristics based on users' perceptions. This more encompassing definition is generally analogous to that used in the study discussed previously about the use of and attitudes toward social-science information by federal agency decision-makers.

In part, the narrower definition is probably a de facto definition determined by many of the agencies responsible for the conduct of environmental-impact studies.

The federal mandate in the NEPA for SIA is clear, but the commitment of federal agencies is highly variable and uncertain. A primary indicator of agency commitment to SIA is budget allocations, and these have been minimal. One effect of such budget restrictions is the limitation of study methods employed and the limitation of data to secondary sources (Friesema & Culhane, 1976). Thus, examples of impact assessment wherein residents and users have participated in the evaluation of alternatives and in the assessment of impacts are minimal. There has been a great reliance on professional or expert judgments. The extent to which these professional or expert judgments are consonant with those of residents and users is open to question and is in itself an issue for study. If the definition of "social" is extended to include cultural, value, and aesthetic impacts as well as demographic and institutional impacts, as has been suggested, the assumption that professionals' values and judgments can serve as surrogates for those of residents and users is highly conjectural, particularly in reference to value-oriented and aesthetic impacts.

A review of several hundred Environmental Impact Statements (EIS), with the objective of evaluating the quality of science, particularly social science, found in EISs, sheds additional light on the policy/practice gap (Friesema & Culhane, 1976). The social consequences considered and discussed in the EISs were found to be limited and usually confined to economic consequences. Other findings were that methods were "crude," studies were usually unrelated to social theory, and, in contrast to natural science studies, little primary social-science research was conducted preparatory to the EIS. In summary, the findings indicate that the SIA components were quite inadequate. A number of reasons are suggested: the backgrounds of agency staff members are typically in the natural sciences and greater weight is frequently given to physical elements (air, water, and land) because of a common understanding among the agency staff; the methods employed make it difficult to give useful predictions of social impacts; and, most significantly, frequently the EIS is written after much planning is done rather than being used as a device for developing alternative plans and concurrent evaluative procedures.

This kind of NEPA policy/practice gap has also been attributed to the basic motivation of agencies and institutions for survival (Cortner, 1976). The survival of institutions is related to the mission of the agency, as defined by Congressional statute. The successful performance of that statutory mission leads to continuing support in the form of budget appropriations. Following this argument, if an agency is charged with the mission of building dams, floodwalls, and other structural measures to control floods or to build highways, its future survival is dependent on its success in building such structures and not on the quality of the EISs it produces. The NEPA calls for a change in agency behavior, but not a change in specific agency mission. Legislation calling for changes in the structure, organization, or behavior of agencies is more difficult to implement. Because NEPA has called for innovative and creative approaches involving the risk of failure, it has not been uniformly or enthusiastically pursued by many agencies. Nevertheless, with the consumer orientation of the NEPA, over time the kinds of changes in agency behavior implicit in the policy are gradually occurring, and more innovative and creative approaches to planning are being pursued.

ONE APPROACH TO CLOSING THE GAP

What is the state-of-the-art in environmental perception, and how might this present level be a contribution to the policy/practice gap? Table 3-3 presents estimates of the state-of-the-art across a broad range of environmental domains (Craik & Zube, 1975). These estimates are related to a set of five research issues and are derived from a series of research workshops involving federal and state decision-makers, researchers from several disciplines, and professional practitioners (for example, designers, planners, and consulting scientists). The purpose of the research workshops was to identify the information needed to develop a systematic approach to using user-based perceptions in environmental decision-making or, in other words, to enhance the utility of social-science data. As indicated in Table 3–3, the state-of-the-art was estimated to be highly variable among domains and issues.

In preparation for the workshops, the five issues were rephrased as the following questions and addressed to leading researchers in each environmental domain:

1. Is there evidence on the viability of the distinction between preferential judgments and comparative appraisals?
2. Is there evidence on the degree of consensus among individuals and groups in appraising environmental quality?
3. Is there evidence on the degree of agreement between experts and laypersons in their appraisals of environmental quality?
4. Is there evidence for other extraenvironmental, observer-related correlates (for example, familiarity, social class) of variations in environmental quality appraisals?
5. Is there evidence on the degree and kinds of relationships obtaining between observer-based appraisals of environmental quality and pertinent physical environmental quality indices?
6. Is there other evidence that bears upon the feasibility of developing standard PEQIs (Perceived Environmental Quality Indices) (Craik & Zube, 1976, p. 10)?

The first question relates to an important conceptual issue, the distinction between preferential judgments that are entirely personal, subjective responses to specific environments, and comparative appraisals that judge the relative quality of specific environments against implicit or explicit standards of comparison. If there is a distinction, one would expect to find greater consensus among individuals on comparative appraisals than on preferential judgments. Such a distinction also has obvious significance for decision-makers in considering the utility of social-science information.

The concept of comparative appraisals and preferential judgments is analogous to the concept of place-centered and person-centered evaluations introduced in Chapter 1. Both comparative appraisals and place-centered evaluations are hypothesized to invoke a normative or standard scale of quality among users, while preferential judgments and person-centered evaluations invoke the purely

Table 3–3. Research State-of-the-Art: Estimates*

Research Issues	Environmental Contexts					Environmental Media			
	Urban Environment	Natural Environment (Scenery)	Recreational Environment	Residential Environments	Institutional Environments	Air	Water	Sound	Land
Distinction between comparative appraisals and preferential judgments	None	Some	None	Some	None	None	None	None	None
Consensus among individuals and groups	Little	Some	Some	Some	Little	Some	Little	Considerable	None
Agreement between experts and laypersons	Little	Considerable	Some	Some	Little	Little	None	None	None
Relationships between observer-based appraisals and physical indices	Little	Considerable	Considerable	Some	Little	Some	Little	Considerable	None
Feasibility studies of developing standard perceived environmental quality indices	None	Some	Some	Little	Little	None	None	Considerable	None

*From *Issues in Perceived Environmental Quality Research*, by K. H. Craik and E. H. Zube. Copyright 1975 by the University of Massachusetts. Reprinted by permission of The Environmental Institute, University of Massachusetts at Amherst.

personal qualitative standards of individual users. The hypothesized lower variability among responses that should result from the former coupled with the notion of explicit or implicit normative or standard qualitative scales are important conditions for increasing the utility of aggregate perceptual data.

The second question addresses the issue of variability independently from the first question. As indicated in Table 3-3, a good bit more research has been done on this question than on the first, but with the exception of research on sound or noise, work on most domains is modest at best.

The third question addresses the issue of variability in responses between experts and laypersons, or users. Do users agree with decision-makers, scientists, planners, and designers?

The fourth question addresses the relationship between perceptions of the environment and variables such as familiarity with the environment, education, income, and communications media. What are the effects of such variables on users' perceptions?

The fifth question addresses the relationship between perceptions of the environment and characteristics of the physical environment. Are there salient physical dimensions of the environment correlated with perceptions of quality? Information on physical correlates provides a basis for making more informed decisions about environmental modifications to meet environmental quality goals and objectives for establishing standards and guidelines. This question addresses the issue of using perceptually based information on the quality of the environment in the development of indices (for example, an aggregation of measurements conveying information about the quality of some environmental domain or element) that could be used in conjunction with physically based environmental indices.

Question six asks if there is other evidence indicating the feasibility of developing PEQIs. Several additional insights into the state-of-the-art can be deduced from Table 3-3. First, there is considerable variability across questions in reference to research emphasis. Notable is the lack of research relating to the distinction between comparative appraisals and preferential judgments, and to consensus among individuals and groups. And, second, there is considerable variability across environmental domains (context and media), with the greatest emphasis on natural environments (scenic), recreational environments, and sound.

The impetus for much of the research on natural and recreational environments can be traced to the considerable body of policy promulgated during the 1960s relating to aesthetics and recreation, and to the environmental impact requirements of the NEPA. Scenic rivers (Dearinger, 1968; Leopold, 1969; Morisawa, 1971), scenic trails (Shafer & Mietz, 1969), and scenic highways (Jones & Jones, 1974) provided policy-relevant settings for research. Forest management for esthetics and recreation (Daniel & Boster, 1976) provided another policy-relevant issue. Additional efforts were initiated in response to the concern with aesthetic impacts of energy facilities (Battelle, 1974), and the identification of scenic values as a component of resource-planning programs (Zube, 1976).

Perceptual research on the sonic environment has undoubtedly been stimulated by the highly subjective nature of human responses. The use of various scales of dissatisfaction (for example, annoyance) is frequent in assessing responses to changes in sonic environments such as those brought about by freeway construction and airport expansion projects (Weinstein, 1976). Much of the field research on sound is related to environmental impact assessments for such construction and expansion in projects.

A long list of recommendations resulted from the workshops for improving the state-of-the-art, thereby helping to close the policy/practice gap—at least in some respects. In general, these recommendations address issues of standardizing measurement procedures for perceived environmental quality, the adequacy of measurements with particular regard to test/retest reliability and the validity of the measurements, and the influences of social-system variables on perceived environmental quality.

SUMMARY

What, then, is the nature of the policy/practice gap as it relates to user-based environmental evaluation? It appears that the gap has a number of components: problems of communications and agreement among decision-makers, scientists, planners, designers, and users; decision-makers' perceptions of social/behavioral scientists as naive with respect to policy-related issues; uneven support by agencies of specific legislative mandates calling for social-science contributions; and an uneven and uncoordinated research base in environmental perception. There is also a positive side to the question that is found in some agency practices and in specific efforts to close the gap. The trend of state legislatures toward establishing institutionalized procedures for program evaluation and the reports of upper-level federal decision-makers about their use of social-science data are important positive signs. Efforts by a number of universities to bring together planning, design, and social-science students in interdisciplinary problem-oriented courses represent important grass-roots efforts to bridge the communications gap. And, finally, efforts to coordinate research interests with policy-related issues and to involve decision-makers in the research-planning activity are essential steps toward a further closing of the gap.

CHAPTER EXERCISE

Interview several environmental decision-makers such as the campus planner at your university, the head of the local housing authority or the local or state parks director to learn what kinds of information they use most frequently to aid them in making decisions. If they don't use social-science information, why not? Under what conditions might they? What kind of social-science information would they find most helpful and from which disciplines?

SUPPLEMENTARY READINGS

The supplementary readings recommended for this chapter provide examples of the kinds of information suggested for public decision-makers—information that can be useful in the form of social and environmental quality indicators and social impact data. These readings also provide a review of research needs in social impact assessment and environmental perception.

Craik, K. H., and Zube, E. H. *Perceiving environmental quality, research and applications*. New York: Plenum Press, 1976.
U.S. Department of Commerce. *Social indicators 1976*. Washington, D.C.: Superintendent of Documents, U.S. Government Printing Office, 1977.
Wolf, C. P. (Ed.). *Social impact assessment*. Environmental Design Research Association, Inc., 1974.

Chapter 4

THE PLANNING/DESIGN PROCESS

OPENING UP THE PROCESS

The environmental quality movement, the consumer-orientation of recent public policy, and, in particular, NEPA, are contributing to important changes in the planning/design process. As noted in Chapter 2, important attributes of NEPA that influence planning/design activities include requirements for the consideration of alternatives, the assessment of potential impacts, and the public disclosure of all studies and data relating to a specific project. This chapter investigates several of these changes in greater detail, within the context of a conceptual framework for planning/design decision-making. A traditional planning/design process, or framework, is described first, and is then used as a basis of comparison for the conceptual process. Finally, a brief overview is provided of various modes that have been adopted for opening up the process—that is, for providing opportunities for user participation.

DEFINITIONS

The terms *planning* and *design* should be defined before embarking on descriptions and discussions of the traditional process and the conceptual process. These terms are frequently used to connote differences in geographic scale, level of specificity, and end product. Planning is defined as a large scale, general, objective, more abstract activity that results in guides, administrative policies, and statements of general intent. Design is defined as a smaller scale, specific, more subjective and detailed activity that results in physical changes in the environment (Eckbo, 1969, p. 46). In this context, a city or transportation system is planned, and a subdivision, house, highway, or bridge is designed. As used here, however, the terms are synonymous, and refer to activities that resolve physical environmental needs and problems and provide for conscious change in the environment. The agent of change may be management practices, such as burning lower sulfur-content fuel to improve air quality, or preventing the filling of coastal wetlands in order to protect an important link in the marine food chain; or the agent of change may be more direct physical interventions such as the construction of public housing to meet the needs of low-income families, or a new power generating plant to meet the seemingly ever-increasing need for energy. The term *design* will be used in lieu of the combination term *planning and design,* and is here defined as a rational decision-making process for guiding desired changes that lead to a quality environment.

THE LINEAR PROCESS

A traditional design process is indicated in Figure 4-1. This approach is essentially linear in concept and practice. The term *linear* means that the steps in the process are sequential and there are no feedback loops in the procedure. A linear process does not provide for the development of alternative designs. It represents a more authoritarian concept of how decisions are made, and relies very heavily, if not totally, on professional expertise. The primary role played by the user is that of approving the final design—and this is a role open to the user

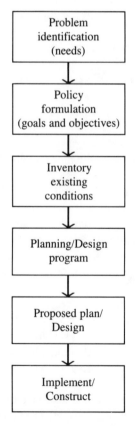

Figure 4-1. Linear design process.

only in specific cases. Relationships tend to be established between the professional and the client who, in the case of most public projects, is not the direct user. Public clients are the local housing authority, park board, or school board, and not the users—that is, the residents of the housing, the visitors to the parks, and the students and teachers. Perceptions of the problem—of the adequacy of existing facilities to meet identified needs and value orientations—can differ in important ways between professionals, manager-clients, and the ultimate users.

The example of planning for college student housing was given in Chapter 1 to illustrate the construct of evaluation. This example is also useful for illustrating the linear design process.

First, it should be recognized that this process provides little or no opportunity for users to participate in the early stages of designing. Values that shape the programs and influence the solution derive primarily from the perceptions and experiences of the college administration. Administrators' values may be biased —for example, toward beliefs about "appropriate" student life-styles, administrative efficiency, or the importance of pleasing the Board of Regents. This is not to say that this process always involves value orientations dissimilar from those of the student users, but it does suggest a strong possibility that such will be the case.

This initial value orientation conditions the identification of goals and the delineation of needs. Goals derived from the values of the decision-makers or the manager-clients will not necessarily consider student satisfaction as a primary goal. Administrative decision-makers are frequently not well enough informed to recognize the salient attributes of satisfaction, or they may consider other goals, such as efficiency and ease of maintenance, more important.

The prevailing, if not exclusive, reliance on the expertise and knowledge of decision-makers carries throughout the process. The inventory of existing conditions will incorporate those attributes and characteristics that relate to the goals and needs of the decision-makers. It may focus in on durable, long-lasting, and easily maintained materials or on spatial arrangements of buildings and rooms believed to foster certain kinds of administratively approved social behavior. A good example of the latter is the notion of placing men's and women's housing on opposite sides of the campus so as to discourage intimate relationships between male and female students. How many campuses still have dormitories located in this way?

The design program limits and directs the process (White, 1972). It is an instrument in which facts and assumptions relating to the realization of the desired environment are organized to provide direction for the development of designs. The program, in written and graphic form, records and organizes information about client needs, and information acquired through the inventory process. It includes facts about physical conditions as well as limitations imposed by codes, laws, and regulations. It should also include social and behavioral facts and information acquired from actual or potential users. "A program is a plan of action for achieving desired results and goals . . ." (White, 1972, p. 11). In the absence of social and behavioral information, the program represents an inaccurate and inappropriately simple plan of action.

The linear process, which is susceptible to overlooking important user-based values and needs, also leads to simplified solutions. Furthermore, it supports the practice of producing the single solution rather than alternative solutions. A single design for a dormitory is produced that relates more to the limited concerns of the client than to the diverse concerns of both client and users. Alternative designs, on the other hand, provide an opportunity to illustrate the differences that emerge when different values and needs are emphasized. Alternative designs may include on- and off-campus locations, and variations in dormitory room arrangements, such as individual rooms, suites, and apartments.

Finally, the oversimplification of the process that is inherent in the linear structure does not foster the idea of feedback. For example, information gleaned from the inventory is not likely to cause a reconsideration of the problem or the needs. If the problem is defined initially as inadequate dormitory space, but the inventory reveals that greater student satisfaction is obtained in nondormitory housing, it is unlikely that the problem will be redefined as inadequate student housing rather than as inadequate dormitory space. The former statement of the problem is much broader and can lead to consideration of a wider range of alternatives than the latter. The linear process also ends with plan implementation or construction of the designed facility. It does not extend to an evaluation of the new environment after it has been used, so that what has been learned can be used to refine the problem, definitions, and policies and contribute to better decisions the next time a similar plan or design is undertaken.

A CONCEPTUAL FRAMEWORK

Figure 4-2 depicts a conceptual framework for the design process that differs in several important ways from the linear process presented in Figure 4-1. First, the process is circular and iterative; second, the final product is derived from the consideration of alternatives; third, evaluation is an explicit component; and, fourth, the process is extended to include a period of use and a feedback loop.

The identification of needs, the inventory activity, and the setting of goals and objectives all interact. The relationships are neither linear nor unidirectional, and the design process may start with any of these steps.

The essential components of the design program, domains, elements, and standards and criteria, were introduced in Chapter 1. These program components make explicit, in physical/environmental terms, the policy goals and objectives. They identify important spatial and temporal relationships, and standards of performance to be expected after implementation of the design. They not only define the parameters of the design in both quantitative and qualitative terms (to the extent possible) but, in so doing, they should also provide the major set of standards and criteria for evaluation. The program components, combined with

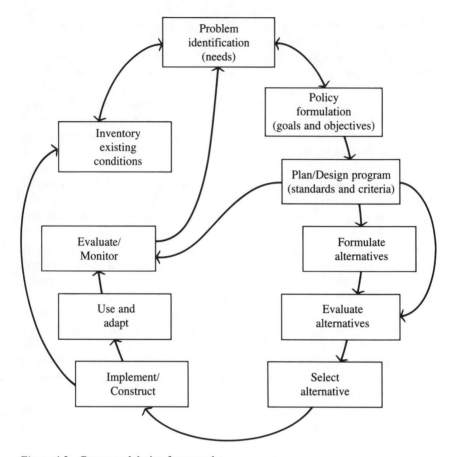

Figure 4-2. Conceptual design framework.

quantitative and qualitative inventory data, are the primary ingredients for the formulation of alternatives. The program defines what is to be. The inventory of existing conditions identifies environmental opportunities and limitations within the context of the identified problem.

The formulation of alternative designs is a circular and iterative process. It involves multiple cycles of design formulation proceeding from general approximations to ever-increasing detail. It is not necessarily a smooth, flowing process however. It can be, and frequently is, sporadic, surging ahead as new information comes to hand, and lagging behind at other times. Each iteration of each alternative is a refining procedure in which the alternative is brought into closer juxtaposition with the program and the opportunities and limitations presented by the existing environmental conditions. In concept, the process is essentially the same whether the problem involves the development of a management plan that meets both timber harvest and aesthetic objectives in ponderosa pine forests, or the design of housing for middle-income families.

The notion of alternatives includes both alternative environments and alternative management devices (for example, management policies). In the example cited above, it includes alternative ways of managing timber harvest and its after-effects so as to minimize, or, if possible, to enhance, the visual impact of logging. In the case of a transportation plan, this concept could include consideration of four or five alternative routes for a new highway to alleviate traffic congestion on an existing commuter road. It could also include alternative means of reducing the congestion problem, such as staggering the starting and quitting times at the commuters' places of employment, or setting aside one lane on the existing highway solely for use as an express lane for a commuter bus system and for cars carrying at least three passengers.

In the case of solving a housing problem, alternative designs might include single-family detached dwellings, townhouses, garden apartments or high-rise apartments, or various combinations of these forms. The alternatives might also be locational—urban, suburban, or rural. Or, alternatives might be in the form of lowered interest rates on mortgage loans, tax incentives to assist developers and to stimulate the construction industry, rezoning of land for higher densities, or rent subsidies to those families and individuals most disadvantaged by the existing housing problem. In other words, the development of alternatives in the design process is intended to encourage consideration of all potentially feasible ways of addressing the identified problem within the value boundaries and related goals and objectives established by public policy.

The impact statement requirements of the NEPA have also served as a stimulus to some federal agencies to incorporate impact assessment procedures into the alternative design formulation process. Inasmuch as the NEPA requires both the consideration of alternatives and an assessment of the effects of maintaining the status quo, the identification of potential impacts as a concurrent rather than a post hoc design activity facilitates the identification and refinement of the most feasible alternatives. This concurrent activity constitutes a continuous, albeit sometimes limited, evaluation throughout the several cycles of alternative formulation. As a result, the impact statement, or report, can be an inherent component of the process.

Evaluation is, in some respects, a continuous activity throughout the conceptual process. It occurs in the inventory of existing conditions, addressing both quantitative and qualitative dimensions of the environment. It is also, as indicated above, an inherent component in the iterative process of formulating and refining alternatives. Two additional evaluations of major importance are included in this process: the evaluation of feasible alternatives that leads to the selection of a design, and, second, the evaluation of an environment after it has been constructed and used, or the monitoring of a managed environment after the design has been implemented and in effect for a period of time.

This concept of evaluation differs considerably from earlier and more traditional approaches, in which the primary emphasis was on an analysis of probable economic benefits and costs. The benefit/cost (B/C) approach to public project evaluation got its start with the Flood Control Act of 1936, in which Congress decreed that water resource development projects could not be implemented unless the benefits (to anyone) exceeded the costs (Krueckeberg & Silvers, 1974, p. 196). B/C analysis, which is a preconstruction activity, is still a part of public project evaluation and is used for a wide array of projects in addition to those concerned with water resources (for example, flood control, navigation, and irrigation), including transportation, energy, and recreation. It is a tool or technique for assessing the economic efficiency of a proposed course of action (Coomber & Biswas, 1973). For our purposes, it is important to note that in spite of its history of over forty years of use, B/C analysis is an inadequate tool for assessing environmental and quality-of-life attributes that are primarily experiential and perceptual in nature.

The various stages in the conceptual process engage a host of participants ranging from administrators and officials to technical experts and laypersons. In many design activities the team of professionals retains a fairly constant make-up throughout the process. The make-up of the citizen-participant body, however, frequently changes over time, with different individuals becoming involved as the process moves from the more general and abstract tasks of defining goals and objectives to the more specific and concrete tasks of evaluating alternatives and, finally, to evaluating and monitoring the resultant environments. Those who participate in the earlier, more abstract stages frequently tend to be so-called "community leaders" (or their counterparts at other levels of government), and tend not to be those who are involved in later evaluation activities focusing on specific environmental modifications of direct interest to potential or actual users. Those who are intellectually attracted to broader, more abstract community, state, or federal policy issues frequently are not as interested in the detailed, concrete plans and designs by which those policies are realized. Or, in the case of college student housing, the students who participated in the initial design stages will no longer be in school at the time the housing is constructed and occupied.

The final characteristic indicated previously as distinguishing this theoretical, conceptual process from the traditional linear process was the feedback loop. The feedback loop is the channel for the final monitoring or evaluation activity. It channels information on the success or failure of designs back into the system so that the efficacy of policy can be assessed, the problem identification can be reconsidered, amended, or redefined, and the design program can be affirmed or revised, if necessary, to include new elements and more demanding or less demanding standards and criteria.

PATTERNS OF PARTICIPATION

The public disclosure aspect of the NEPA contributes to a growing pattern of greater citizen participation in public decision-making. Although there are a number of examples of citizen participation in planning programs, going back a considerable number of years—for example, to the efforts of the Tennessee

Valley Authority and Soil Conservation Service in the 1930s—the nature and intensity of present activities varies considerably from those earlier efforts. The Tennessee Valley Authority effort has been described as one of cooptation—that is, of absorbing individuals into the operation of the Authority so as to subvert potential disagreement with its operation and continued existence (Kasperson & Breitbart, 1974). Citizen participation activities after World War II, however, are generally viewed as having their genesis with urban residents and urban problems. They represent, at least in part, a reaction against previous modes, which usually viewed participation as a means of ensuring the success of a specific plan rather than as a means of identifying problems, evaluating alternatives, and monitoring results. The urban renewal efforts and urban expressway construction of the 1950s, which threatened the housing of low-income families, gave rise to the advocacy planning approaches of the 1960s.

Planners working in the advocacy mode usually represented a specific client group, eschewing the presumably value-free role of the professional planner and, through a closer working relationship with the client group, advocated their values and goals. There have been many criticisms of the advocacy mode, however. Primary concerns are frequently of a protest nature, to stop an action, and seldom of a creative nature, to initiate or support desired change. It is difficult for the advocate to truly represent clients' values and not recast their statements in terms of what he or she thinks they need. And, local groups frequently believe that all problems are susceptible to local solution—a parochial outlook that does not acknowledge external constraints (Porteous, 1977, p. 364).

The Economic Opportunity Act of 1964 represents an important policy bench mark in the movement toward broader public participation in the planning and evaluation of public programs and projects. It called for "maximum feasible participation of residents of the areas and members of the groups served." The Amendments of 1975 specifically identified urban planning and design activities as coming under this mandate, as well as program and project evaluation responsibilities.

Essentially, all of the major environmental legislation passed since the NEPA of 1969 (see Table 2-1) has called for citizen participation in the decision-making process, whether it relates to the development of plans for managing the existing environment or to plans and designs for environmental modification and construction projects. The Clean Air Act Amendments of 1970, Federal Water Pollution Control Act Amendments of 1972, Housing and Urban Development Act of 1970 (and the Amendments of 1975), and the Coastal Zone Management Act of 1972 all call for public involvement in one way or another. The ways in which these requirements have been met vary considerably both in mode and effectiveness, but have tended to rely most heavily on the use of advisory committees and public hearings. Both of these involvement techniques have limitations and advantages. The advisory committee approach usually involves appointed members who are presumed to represent the relevant members of the public and special interest groups. Because much of the planning activity is carried on during the working day and, in some instances, involves travel to meetings at various locations throughout the state or region, there are frequently financial limitations on who is able to participate. Loss of income because of absence from work and the additional costs of travel provide real constraints to participation, and thus to the concept of a representative committee. The committee approach can, however, provide continuity of citizen involvement throughout the duration of a project.

Public hearings are formally structured meetings where anyone who desires can present a statement in public on the issue under consideration. Heberlein (1976) suggests four functions for public hearings: (1) informational—the transfer of information from professionals to citizens; (2) cooptative—the enlisting of citizen support for a chosen course of action; (3) ritualistic—to satisfy the requirements of the law; and (4) interactive—the exchange of views among participants. Disadvantages of the public hearing are that it provides no basis for representativeness and frequently tends to be biased. Proponents for or against an issue can arrange for disproportionate representation, or "stacking" of the hearing. Hearings may exclude those individuals who are self-conscious about or frightened at the prospect of making a public statement. The time and location of the meeting can exclude some citizens from participation. The public nature of the hearing does, however, facilitate the dissemination of information through the news media.

Technical committees, planning workshops, and sample surveys are also employed as vehicles for citizen participation. Technical committees draw on citizens who have expertise relevant to the issue under consideration and are able to provide an "outsider's" opinion and evaluation. Such committees are based on the notion that the citizen-expert would be somewhat independent of any particular value orientation of the planning or design agency. This approach warrants an interdisciplinary committee so as to minimize the effects of professional biases that could and do accrue if the members are of the same profession as those individuals from the agency responsible for the planning and design.

Planning workshops are smaller and less structured than public hearings and provide for interaction among participants. They provide a forum where invited representatives of interest groups can exchange ideas with and comment on alternatives proposed by the agency. Some of the same disadvantages identified with participation on an advisory committee are also relevant here. The lack of representativeness in workshops could be overcome, however, by employing a random selection procedure for participants, much as is done in jury selection, and by making it more possible for all selected individuals to serve by paying them (Heberlein, 1976).

Sample surveys provide the best approach to the problem of representativeness. Finsterbusch (1976) suggests that some of the data needed for social impact assessments for highway locations can be provided only by surveys. In addition to addressing the issue of representativeness, random samples of the general public, or of relevant subgroups of the general public, can be used to determine value orientations and attitudes toward particular issues, and to assess the level of understanding of the issues. Sample surveys can provide useful information to help identify goals and needs, for the evaluation of alternatives, and for the evaluation of completed projects. Disadvantages of the sample survey include the fact that it does not provide for interaction among participants and that it is frequently more expensive than other modes of participation. Also the results can be misleading if the interview schedule is not carefully designed, or if the sample is improperly drawn.

A considerably different approach to the intervention of citizen values in environmental decision-making is represented by the strategy suggested by Sax (1971). Sax, an environmental lawyer, is an advocate of the use of the courts for the resolution of environmental controversies surrounding those issues and actions that reflect value and goal conflicts between special interest groups or between groups and public agencies. He argues that established legal procedures are already at hand, and that the selective use of the courts can do much to ensure citizen participation "as one essential and continuing factor in the search for environmental quality" (Sax, 1971, p. 232). In other words, the threat of a court order can go a long way toward keeping the process open. The precedent-setting aspects of this approach, with the subsequent implications for future actions, is certainly one very great advantage. It is also an approach that requires some knowledge of what kinds of actions are possible under the law, along with access to legal expertise in order to develop and pursue the case. This latter requirement can present a formidable hurdle to those with limited financial means.

Opening up the design process has obviously created a set of implementation problems. How can citizen participation best be accomplished? The record to date is checkered and uneven (Kasperson & Breitbart, 1974; Porteous, 1977). No single approach devised thus far provides a universal answer. Each has advantages and disadvantages. Table 4-1 summarizes some of these critical points for the modes of participation previously discussed, and provides graphic illustration of the absence of a universal mode. There is considerable variability in the issue

Table 4-1. Comparison of Citizen Participation Modes

	Representa- tiveness	Opportunity for Interaction	Opportunity for Continuity	Absence of Economic Constraints
Advisory committee	Med.	High	High	Med.
Public hearing	Low	Low	Low	Med.
Technical committee	Low	High	High	Med.
Planning workshops	Med.	High	High	Med.
Sample surveys	High	Low	Low	High
Legal intervention	Low	High	Low	Low
Advocacy	Med.	Med.	High	Med.

of representation, and in reference to economic constraints on participation. Modes of participation also seem to divide into two relatively distinct groups in reference to opportunities for interaction between professionals and citizens and opportunities for continuity of involvement by citizens throughout the design process—from problem-identification to the monitoring of resultant environmental changes.

The problem of who participates, and how, is central to the evolution of a more democratically based design process. It is highly unlikely, however, that a process totally open at every step and fully democratic with regard to every decision can ever be developed. Our society is still composed of a majority of nonparticipants, and that situation is unlikely to change. It is also questionable whether such a process would be desirable, as it would undoubtedly be unwieldy and create interminable delays in decision-making.

An open planning process, to be successful, must be highly flexible. Wilkinson (1976) suggests that there are three functional categories of citizen participation: education/information, review/reaction, and interaction/dialogue. These three categories can include a range of participation mechanisms. The mechanism(s) must be selected that best fit the task at hand, and no one mechanism fits all tasks.

EVALUATION COMPONENTS OF THE CONCEPTUAL DESIGN PROCESS

The preceding discussion indicates that evaluation occurs, in one form or another, in many stages of the conceptual process. The interest here, however, is not with the evaluative decisions made by professionals within the iterative process of alternative formulation, as important as they are, but rather with evaluation as a specific kind of citizen participation activity. For the results of this activity to have maximum utility for decision-makers, special attention must be directed to the design and conduct of the evaluation components of the process. Decision-makers' concerns about objectivity, reliability, and validity (see Chapter 2) suggest that this aspect of the process be cast in the form of applied research.

Recognizing that environmental design is art as much as science, and sometimes mostly art, evaluations that adopt a scientific mode ensure the highest probability of utility. This, then, indicates that some of the traditional modes of citizen participation, discussed earlier in this chapter, are not the most suitable for the evaluation stages.

Advisory committees, public hearings, and planning workshops are useful ways to obtain information from organized sectors of the public, from economically able, public-spirited individuals, the "professional citizens" who are repeat participators, or those who feel threatened by possible changes. They can also provide an important forum for profession/citizen interaction, but they are rarely representative and frequently yield biased contributions to the design process. The perceptions of decision-makers about valid and reliable techniques for obtaining social-science information—systematic observation, survey research, and field experiments—provide important and rational guidance for evaluation studies and lend strong support for the adoption of an applied research model and a quasi-experimental strategy whenever possible. Sommer (1973) refers to such an applied research model as an "evaluation model" and distinguishes it from a basic research model, in that the latter "seems to deal with immutable laws and relationships about abstract categories of individuals—schizophrenics, alcoholics, old people, young people, and so on. Evaluation deals with a specific, concrete situation and the people actually in it—the tenants in the Bedford-Stuyvesant housing project, campers in Yosemite, or people living in the Ohio River floodplain" (p. 129).

The experimental design is one in which the researcher attempts to control all variables and allows only one to vary in a specified manner. Subjects are selected at random and assigned to groups at random. Experimental treatments are randomly assigned to these groups. This procedure provides for maximum clarity on points of internal validity—that is, on the effects of the treatments. It can be assumed that measurable changes are caused by the specified variation in a single variable. Such conditions do not exist outside of the laboratory. Quasi-experimental designs, in which randomization and control of treatments is not possible but in which measures are repeated so as to assess changes over time (time series), or within and among different groups (comparisons), can provide a useful strategy for environmental evaluation. Recognizing the limitations of internal validity imposed by such a design, it is suggested that there may be an advantage in terms of external validity, or, in other words, to the generalizability of the findings to other groups and situations (Cook & Campbell, 1975). For example, Campbell has suggested that if the slum clearance programs of the 1930s had been evaluated using quasi-experimental designs, the high-rise housing projects of the 1950s and 1960s probably would not have been built (Salasin, 1973, p. 7).

The quasi-experimental design provides for the control of at least one independent variable, such as time and/or type of setting. It provides for comparison among settings—for example, satisfaction ratings among three different housing designs, or aesthetic ratings among different sections of a regional landscape, or comparison of findings from the same setting at different times, such as worker satisfaction before and after the remodeling of an office space.

The quantitative, quasi-experimental approach to evaluation accommodates a wide range of social and behavioral science methods, including attitudinal surveys, systematic observation and the use of checklists, rating scales, and ranking procedures—all of which have considerable potential for evaluational data gathering (Lang, Burnette, Moleski & Vachon, 1974; Michelson, 1975). Of particular significance to decision-makers is the explicit nature of the approach, which offers the opportunity to make limitations clear.

It is important to note that several criticisms of this approach have been advanced. For example, the time spans involved in gathering time-series data are frequently viewed as excessive by political policy-makers, who relate to a two- or four-year election cycle and expect findings to be advanced in much shorter time periods. This is not a problem, however, with designs that compare across settings. When undue reliance is placed on methods that involve self-reports by participants, the question of the relationship between what people say they do and what they actually do is raised. This is a clearly justifiable concern, and calls for the employment of multiple methods so as to provide cross-checks on perceptual and experientially oriented data. These issues are illustrated by example in Chapters 5, 6, and 7.

Whichever model and methods are used, they have to be adapted to the specific evaluation task at hand—inventory, selection among alternatives, or assessment of the quality of new environments. These three tasks can be divided into two major and generally distinctive categories of study, each of which presents some unique challenges in study design, as well as having common characteristics. The first category relates both to the inventory stage and to the post-use and adaptation stage of evaluation and monitoring. It involves the evaluation of existing environments in both the pre- and post-design conditions. It therefore involves a degree of reality achieved through direct experience of the subject environments. This is one of the major factors differentiating this category from the second.

The second category involves the evaluation of possible future environments, and the experiential effects or impacts associated with those alternative futures. In the first category, the physical environment exists, is tangible, and can be experienced. In the second category, the primary reference point is the existing pre-design condition. The proposed alternatives have to be perceived on some other basis. Salient domains and elements may be communicated by means of simulations, such as models and drawings, by verbal descriptions, or by reference to analogs. The proposed alternatives may include experiences not previously shared by those participating in the evaluation and/or the potential users. The evaluation study must recognize the possibility of participant responses being conditioned by aversion to change, which is associated with the unknown. Thus, the evaluation of alternatives and potential impacts, unless carefully designed, can result in supporting or reinforcing the status quo and stifling creativity in the search for solutions to environmental problems. The previously discussed idea of a distinction between comparative appraisals and preferential judgments (see Chapter 3) may provide a useful framework for addressing this potential problem. This idea suggests that considerable attention be given to the psychological set, or context, for the participants, the nature of the instructions or directions, and the frame of reference provided for the participants in the study.

SUMMARY

Changes in public values and policy are gradually bringing about a transition from a linear design process to a more flexible, interactive, and iterative process referred to here as "the conceptual process," which includes multiple opportunities for citizen participation at various stages. Many of the traditional techniques of citizen participation fail to provide information that meets the tests of reliability and validity sought by administrators and decision-makers. Citizen participation is particularly important to the evaluative stages of the design process. Thus, techniques such as sample surveys, which offer a higher probability of representing the values of all relevant public groups, are needed in these stages.

Two distinctive categories of citizen-oriented evaluative activities have been identified. The first involves the evaluation of existing environments, environments which can be evaluated on the basis of users' direct perceptions and experiences. This includes both the inventory stage and the postconstruction or postimplementation stages of the design process. The second category involves the evaluation of alternative futures, of environments to be created and for which potential users may or may not have an experiential basis to draw on for their evaluative responses. These categories are addressed in some detail in the following three chapters.

CHAPTER EXERCISE

Using a number of problem statements from design studios (architecture, landscape architecture, and interior design), prepare an analysis of the content with specific attention to standards or criteria for evaluation of alternatives and evaluation of the project after completion and an initial period of use. List and organize the qualities and attributes that might be considered in the evaluation. Interview students in the studios working on the problems, if it is a class in which you are not involved. What are the designer's assumptions about patterns of use and user responses? Can these assumptions be stated as criteria for evaluation, including an evaluation of the validity of the assumptions? If the problem statement does not contain standards or criteria relating to user satisfaction and users' perceptions of aesthetic qualities, or if these criteria are vaguely stated, how could the problem statement be changed so that it makes more explicit the design intentions and so that it can be used as a basis for evaluation?

Attend several citizen-participation meetings as an observer. Take notes on how the meeting was organized, who attended, who participated, and what the nature of the participation was (for example, statements of opinion, discussions among interested parties, formal presentations by agency or governmental officials). Analyze your observational data and prepare a report on the effectiveness of the meetings with specific reference to questions of representativeness and opportunity for interaction.

SUPPLEMENTARY READINGS

The following two volumes provide excellent reviews of the relationships between science and environmental planning. Porteous emphasizes the urban environment and the planning process. Saarinen encompasses urban, rural, and wildlands environments, as well as geographic scale considerations ranging from the environment of a single room to towns, cities, regions, and nations.

Porteous, J. D. *Environment and behavior: Planning and everyday urban life.* Reading, Mass.: Addison-Wesley, 1977.
Saarinen, T. F. *Environmental planning: Perception and behavior.* Boston: Houghton Mifflin, 1976.

Chapter 5

EVALUATING EXISTING ENVIRONMENTS

WHY EVALUATE EXISTING ENVIRONMENTS?

Existing environments are evaluated early in the design process, as suggested in Chapter 4, for several related but nevertheless distinctive reasons: (1) to identify the status quo or to obtain base-line data on the quality of the environment prior to the development of plans for modification; (2) to identify existing problems or needs—their characteristics, location, and magnitude; (3) to monitor the quality of the environment over time; and (4) to provide a basis for predicting the quality of future environments.

The purpose of this chapter is to investigate, through the use of selected studies, some of the important issues and concerns of evaluating existing environments. Two studies are included that address the goals of providing and maintaining aesthetic and satisfying environments. The first study, a coastal zone inventory, is concerned primarily with aesthetics, and is responsive to the Coastal Zone Management Act of 1972. The second study, which actually encompasses a series of studies, is an evaluation of city streets. It is concerned with neighborhood satisfaction, and is responsive to both urban development and transportation policies. The chapter concludes with an analysis of the two studies, utilizing the evaluation schema introduced in Chapter 1 as a structuring device for the discussion. This schema will also be used in the following chapters for analyzing studies of alternative future environments and post-construction evaluations.

The schema consists of three dimensions: institutional, environmental, and participatory. The institutional dimension includes the aims or purpose of the study, the agency(s) for whom the data are intended, the person(s) who conduct the study, and how the study is financed. The environmental dimension includes consideration of specific environmental policies, related goals and objectives as expressed in standards and criteria for evaluation, identification of relevant environmental domains, and related physical attributes and characteristics. The participatory dimension includes identification of the appropriate user-roles, the identification of participants or users and, where appropriate, of nonparticipants. It also includes delineation of significant group and individual characteristics.

A COASTAL ZONE PLANNING INVENTORY[1]

The Coastal Zone Management Act of 1972 calls for the consideration of aesthetic, economic, and environmental values in the development of management programs for the coastal zones of designated states and territories. Section 303b of the Act declares a national policy to:

> . . . encourage and assist the states to exercise their responsibilities in the coastal zone through the development of management programs that achieve wise use of land and water resources by giving full consideration to ecological, cultural, historic, and esthetic values as well as to needs for economic development.

The Act directs attention to the importance of aesthetic values (in addition to others) in the designation of shoreline areas of particular concern, especially those for preservation and restoration, and in the selection of lands to be acquired for public shoreline access. Furthermore, the final rules and regulations for program development issued by the Office of Coastal Zone Management (OCZM) suggest that, in determining shoreline access requirements, states and territories should consider visual as well as physical access. In other words, the public should be able to see the shoreline as well as physically use it for recreation. OCZM requirements also note the importance of developing appropriate procedures and criteria for assessing scenic importance.

An important element of the Act is the requirement for citizen participation in the planning process. Considerable latitude is provided with respect to the form and extent of participation that can be employed. The minimum requirement is a public hearing, near the end of the planning process, for the presentation and discussion of the recommended plan. As noted in Chapter 4, this form of participation has serious limitations if it is the only mode employed.

A number of states and territories did go well beyond the minimal requirements (for example, Massachusetts and the U.S. Virgin Islands). Technical or scientific advisory committees, citizen advisory committees, newsletters with "mail-back" questionnaires, and discussion meetings with special interest groups were some of the participation modes most frequently used.

The case study presented below describes a user-based aesthetic evaluation of the coastal zone of the U.S. Virgin Islands. A random-sample household survey was employed to address four topics: scenic quality, coastal problems, shoreline use, and coastal protection.

---

[1] Portions of this case study appear in *Coastal Zone 78* as "Assessing Perceived Values of the Coastal Zone," by E. H. Zube and M. McLaughlin, 1978, Vol. 1, 360–371. Reproduced by permission of the American Society of Civil Engineers.

The Virgin Islands Landscape

Coastal aesthetic resources are of particular importance in the Virgin Islands. Not only do they enhance the well-being of local residents, but they are one of the territory's main tourist attractions (Virgin Islands Planning Office, 1977a).

The three islands are quite distinct in character and form. Despite a rugged and irregular shoreline, the island of St. Thomas is well developed, with houses climbing the hillsides above the main harbors and bays. St. John, the site of Virgin Islands National Park, has comparable topography but is sparsely developed. St. Croix is comparable to St. Thomas in terms of population, but is greater in size and has large areas of more gentle topography. The apparent impact of development is, therefore, lessened considerably. The landscape of St. Croix also includes heavy industry, but, in general, the long, linear shoreline is backed by rolling fields and hills accented by occasional structures.

The territory's coastal zone includes many islands and cays; it is the setting for considerable boating activity, and extensive displays of wave action generated by barrier reefs are common. Below the surface of the Caribbean, scenery of a different sort is found, including reef formations of great variety and complexity teeming with fish and other marine life. Buck Island Reef National Monument near St. Croix is internationally recognized for underwater beauty.

Coastal Environments

A major structuring element of the Virgin Islands planning process was the concept of coastal environments, which was used to classify the coastal zone for inventory and planning purposes. Coastal environments were defined by biophysical characteristics, including slope, surface material (that is, soil, mud, reef, sand, boulders, rock), vegetation, and building development. Primary coastal environments identified were: steep relief/rocky shores, low relief/rocky shores, salt pond, beach, mangrove, developed bays and shorelines, grass beds/algal plains, sand bottoms, coral reef/algal ridges, offshore islands and cays, and open water.

This coastal taxonomy provided a framework for assessing the probable impacts of various development activities. For example, the susceptibility of various environments to erosion, sedimentation, and water pollution suggests limitations for certain uses and appropriateness for others. High- or low-relief rocky shores with highly erodable soils, for example, would probably be rated more appropriate for low-density residential development than for high-density residential or industrial development. Low-density residential development would disturb less of the existing vegetative cover, expose less bare soil, and cover less of the area with pavement, thus reducing the probabilities of increased runoff and associated erosion.

This same coastal taxonomy was used in the design of a household survey, to provide a common environmental unit for comparing user-based data with biophysical resource data. The survey, however, addressed only the landward or terrestrial environments of high relief/rocky shores, low relief/rocky shores, salt ponds, beaches, mangroves, and developed bays and shorelines. Questions relating to three of the four major topics covered in the survey—scenic quality, shoreline use, and coastal protection—were formulated in such a way that responses related directly to the coastal environments.

Users/Residents

Between 1960 and 1976 the population of the U.S. Virgin Islands nearly tripled, increasing from about 32,000 to 95,000 inhabitants. About 60% of this increase is estimated to be attributable to immigration. Most migrants come from nearby Caribbean Islands, and some from the continental United States. This rate of growth, largely associated with a greatly expanded tourist industry, as well as with some industrial development (for example, alumina processing and oil refining on St. Croix), has created not only a larger population, but a more diverse population in terms of place of origin, education, occupation, and income. It has also contributed to the notion of multiple value-orientations toward the island environment, most often expressed as continentals and/or off-islanders (that is, recent migrants) versus natives. Furthermore, there is a feeling that values vary among the populations of the three major islands. In part, this assumed variation may be because of differences in population composition, with St. Croix having a significant number of Spanish-speaking migrants from Puerto Rico. These notions of multiple and variable value-orientations merited investigation if plans were to be developed responsive to the perceived values and needs of coastal zone users and island residents.

The Household Survey

A household survey was designed to gather data on residents' perceptions of and attitudes toward the Virgin Islands coastal zone (Virgin Islands Planning Office, 1977a). Survey objectives were both informational and educational. The primary objectives were to obtain a perceptually based inventory of the coastal zone and information on residents' attitudes toward development in the coastal zone. It was also recognized that engaging residents of the three islands in a survey about coastal issues would provide many participants with new information or, at the very least, cause them to attend consciously to issues they might not otherwise have attended to. Thus, another objective, albeit indirect, was to use the survey as a participatory and educational device contributing to a greater awareness of coastal issues among a representative sample of the population.

In addition to obtaining pertinent background information on the participants, the survey addressed four major topics. The first topic was coastal aesthetics. Of concern were the kinds of shorelines most highly valued for their scenery, and the extent of agreement among individuals, groups, and island populations on the scenic evaluation of the shorelines of each of the three islands. The second topic was perception of the comparative importance of coastal problems, such as beach access, water pollution, flooding, loss of natural areas, sand removal from beaches, and decreasing seafood harvests. The third topic encompassed attitudes toward alternative shoreline uses—industrial, commercial, residential, recreational, and conservation. The fourth topic was perceived need for shoreline protection from development. Two aspects of this fourth topic were of concern: First, was there recognition of the need, and potential support for, shoreline protection programs? Second, if there was a perceived need, what were the reasons given?

The survey was designed by the planning staff and their consultants. The majority of the staff were white continentals employed by the planning office. The actual household survey in the field was conducted by native West Indians.

Photographs of coastal environments, mounted on 11 inch by 16 inch panels, were used in support of the interview questions. One panel of fifteen color photographs depicted representative coastal environments from the three islands (see Figure 5-1). Three panels of fifteen colored photographs each, depicting areas from individual islands, were also prepared. Each coastal environment was shown, to the extent possible, with and without some form of development, such as beaches with and without hotels and high relief/rocky shorelines with and without residential development. A panel of ten black and white photographs (see Figure 5-2) was also prepared, which depicted representative coastal uses (industrial, commercial, residential, recreational, conservation). Each interview involved the use of three panels: (1) color photographs from the three islands; (2) color photographs from the island on which the interview was being conducted; and (3) black and white photographs of coastal uses.

Background data collected on each respondent included sex, age, length of residency in the territory, education, and occupation. These are important variables—in addition to island of residence—with respect to testing the several notions on multiple value-orientations.

Approximately 800 household interviews were planned—about 360 each on St. Croix and St. Thomas, and the balance on St. John. Both St. Croix and St. Thomas have somewhat more than 40,000 inhabitants. The sampling of households was stratified on each island by designating sub-areas on the basis of relatively homogeneous physical and demographic characteristics, and in orientation to particular coastal or urban areas. Random samples were drawn proportional to sub-area populations.

Seven hundred and forty-three interviews were completed—348 on St. Croix, 56 on St. John, and 339 on St. Thomas.

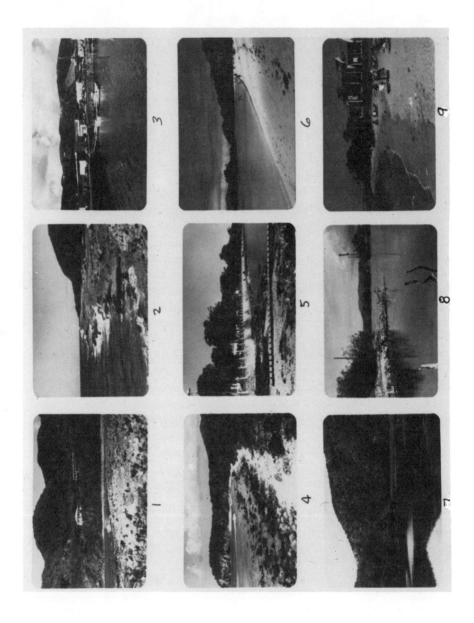

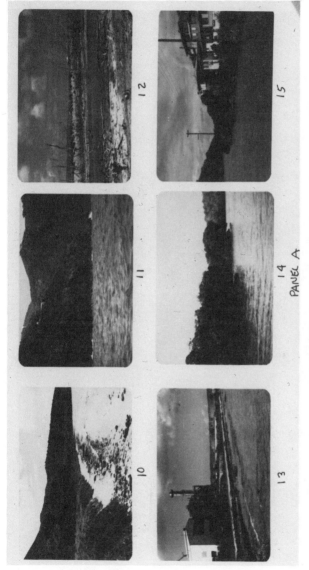

Figure 5-1. Representative coastal environments from St. Croix, St. John, and St. Thomas.

Recreation

Conservation

Figure 5-2. Representative coastal uses, from top to bottom: industry, commerce, residential, recreation, conservation—open space.

A Sample of the Findings

Some important areas of agreement and disagreement emerged from the survey, suggesting multiple value-orientations. These value orientations were not found to vary, however, as a function of the native/continental (or native/non-native) dichotomy, but, rather, as a function of education and island of residence. There was strong agreement among respondents on what shorelines are most scenic, on the importance of protecting some coastal environments, and on the necessity of improving beach access.

With regard to priorities among economic, environmental, and amenity values, however, there was notable variability. The more highly educated respondents favored conservation and recreational development, while those with less formal education tended to favor economic development. The kind of economic development favored among this group also varied somewhat by island of residence, and tended to reflect differences in existing island resources and feasibility of development options. For example, industrial development, which was favored somewhat on St. Croix and St. Thomas, was less favored on St. John, which has very little suitable land for industry, and more difficult access.

Participants in the household survey were asked to identify depicted shorelines that they perceived as most beautiful and as least beautiful—from their home island and from all three islands. Sand beaches, both developed and undeveloped, high-relief rocky shorelines, and mangroves were ranked high. Undeveloped salt ponds, rocky beaches, and dead mangroves were rated among the

Table 5-1. Perceptions of Shoreline Beauty*

Photo No.	Coastal Environment	$\bar{x}$	S.D.	Rank Order
1	Steep Rocky (dev.)	3.10	0.60	10
2	Steep Rocky (undev.)	2.92	0.77	7
3	Developed: Harbor	2.86	0.72	6
4	Rocky Beach (undev.)	3.32	0.85	12
5	Developed: Harbor	2.74	0.77	5
6	Sand Beach (undev.)	1.85	0.87	1
7	Salt Pond (undev.)	3.21	0.76	11
8	Salt Pond (undev.)	3.51	0.73	14
9	Sand Beach (dev.)	2.45	0.74	3
10	Rocky Beach (undev.)	3.03	0.76	9
11	Steep Rocky (dev.)	2.73	0.70	4
12	Dead Mangroves	4.17	0.93	15
13	Developed: Industrial	3.43	0.85	13
14	Mangroves (undev.)	2.39	0.81	2
15	Salt Pond (dev.)	2.97	0.75	8

N = 743

*In response to these questions: "Looking at this panel, which four shorelines are the most beautiful?" "Which of the four is the most beautiful?" "Which four shorelines do you find least beautiful?" "Which is the least beautiful?"

least beautiful. Table 5-1 shows the responses of 743 participants (means—x̄ and standard deviations—S.D.) to questions of aesthetic quality related to the representative sample of coastal environments from the three islands. Photo number in the table refers to the numbers of the individual photographs in Figure 5-1. Inter-island agreement on aesthetic quality was, in general, very high.

Respondents were asked to indicate which types of depicted shorelines should be protected from over-development, and which types were most suitable for conservation, recreation, residences, commerce, and industry. The panel of black and white photographs (see Figure 5-2) was used as a visual model to provide pictorial definitions of these five use categories. Most respondents perceived the following shoreline-use relationships for the three islands:

1. Conservation—undeveloped sand beaches and mangroves
2. Recreation—undeveloped and developed sand beaches
3. Residences—developed and high-relief rocky shorelines and salt ponds
4. Commerce—developed sand beaches and harbors
5. Industry—developed harbors (existing industry) and dead mangrove areas

When shorelines were identified as needing protection, respondents were asked why such areas should be protected. The open-ended responses were coded as shown in Table 5-2.

In general, the findings on respondents' attitudes toward protection were consonant with the uses deemed most suitable for the various coastal environments on the basis of the potential biophysical impact analysis. One important exception emerged, however: perceptions of salt ponds. While salt ponds are not perceived by respondents as either very beautiful or as suitable for conservation —but, rather, as suitable for residential development—they are important as habitat, both for certain endangered species of wading birds and for other wildlife. They are also important as natural sediment traps for storm-water runoff from adjacent lands. Thus, there is a potential conflict between residents' percep-

Table 5-2. Rationale for Shoreline Protection*

Reason	St. Croix N = 228	St. Thomas N = 157	St. John N = 17	Territory N = 402
Ecological value	30.6%	10.1%	26.4%	21.2%
Recreational value	27.1	3.8	5.2	16.0
Scenic value	35.2	49.7	36.9	41.5
Prevent pollution	7.1	4.3	5.2	5.9
Like it as it is	0.0	23.1	21.1	11.1
Already too developed	0.0	9.1	5.2	4.3

*In response to the question: "Why do you feel these areas should be protected?"
Note: Column totals may not equal 100% due to rounding $x^2 = 286.30$, $p \leq .001$ with df = 10.

tions and professional judgments about appropriate environmentally based management policies. This provides a warning signal to planners and others charged with responsibility for plan-implementation.

EVALUATING CITY STREETS

The quality of the urban environment has been the subject of public policy for over forty years. It has been addressed in a number of ways, ranging from the slum clearance provisions of the Housing Act of 1937, through the Interstate Highway and Defense Act of 1956, the new communities provisions of the Housing and Urban Development Act of 1970 (see Chapter 2), to the Supplemental Housing Authorization Act of 1977. This latter act created the National Commission on Neighborhoods, charged with making recommendations for the preservation and rebuilding of neighborhoods of diverse character, and with encouraging public participation in the process. One potentially important component of the quality of urban neighborhoods is the impact of vehicular traffic on the perceptions and experiences of street residents.

Street Livability

Appleyard (1976) undertook a series of studies to identify social and environmental factors related to residents' satisfaction or dissatisfaction with city streets. The Street Livability Study, initiated in 1969, the first in the series, was exploratory—in the nature of a pilot study.

Twelve residents on each of three blocks in San Francisco were interviewed, and pedestrian and traffic activities were observed on the same blocks. The three streets selected were very similar in appearance, but differed markedly in traffic volume, from a light flow of 2000 vehicles per day (VPD), to a medium flow of 8700, and, finally, to a heavy flow of 15,750 VPD (see Figure 5-3). The issues explored in the interviews included: traffic hazard; stress, including noise and air pollution; privacy and sense of territory; neighboring and visiting; and environmental awareness (see Figures 5-4 and 5-5).

The results of this exploratory study led to the formulation of several hypotheses for future testing (Appleyard, 1976, p. 23):

1. Heavy traffic activity might be associated with more apartment renters and fewer owner/occupants and families with children.
2. Heavy traffic is associated with much less social interaction and street activity. Conversely, a street with little traffic and many families promotes a rich social climate and a strong sense of community.
3. Heavy traffic is associated with a withdrawal from the physical environment. Conversely, residents of a street with low traffic show an acute, critical, and appreciative awareness of and care for the physical environment.

Figure 5-3. From top to bottom: light, medium and heavy streets where interviews were taken. (From *Liveable Urban Streets: Managing Auto Traffic in Neighborhoods,* by D. Appleyard. Washington, D.C.: U.S. Government Printing Office, 1976.)

Street Life and Traffic Volume

The second study in the series, undertaken in 1974, included over 400 interviews and a wider range of streets. It provided an opportunity to test the hypotheses developed from the Street Livability Study. The streets were selected to control for certain variables, as follows (Appleyard, 1976, p. 31):

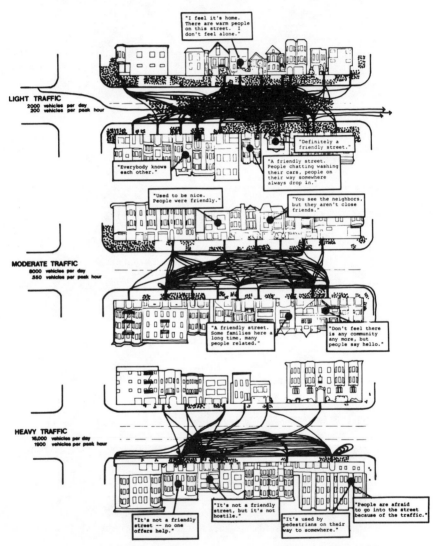

Figure 5-4. Neighboring and visiting. (From *Liveable Urban Streets: Managing Auto Traffic in Neighborhoods*, by D. Appleyard. Washington, D.C.: U.S. Government Printing Office, 1976.)

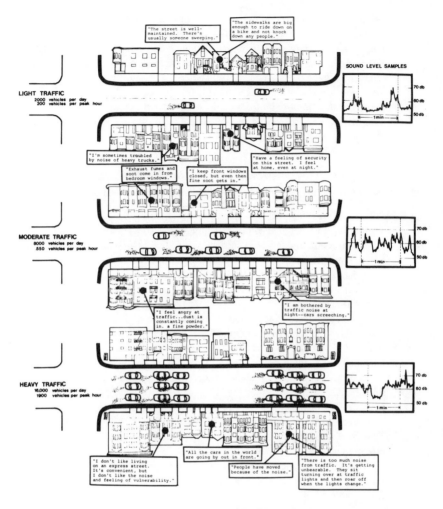

Figure 5-5. Noise, stress and pollution. (From *Liveable Urban Streets: Managing Auto Traffic in Neighborhoods,* by D. Appleyard. Washington, D.C.: U.S. Government Printing Office, 1976.)

1. *Only streets in the inner suburbs.* Because residential traffic problems are more likely to be severe in the inner city where densities are higher and streets narrower, we decided to concentrate on inner city situations.
2. *Only streets in San Francisco.* Limiting the streets to those in San Francisco saved on travel expenses and secondary data collection, for traffic, accidents, land values, and census data could be gathered more easily. Climatic differences with cities that have severe winters will limit the generality of the findings with respect to the effects of climate, such as snowfall, plowing, and slush problems, and conditions of excessive heat when more people are forced out of doors or

behind air conditioners. Wind and rain San Francisco has. The climate is cool with approximately four months of rainy season in winter.

3. *Only flat or slightly sloping streets.* Although San Francisco is a city of hills, flat or slightly sloping portions of the streets were selected as a control device, allowing us to be more in keeping with other U.S. cities.

4. *Setbacks.* A range of building setbacks, from those with residences directly on the sidewalk to those with front yards, was selected in each of the major traffic categories. We also looked at the effects of traffic on apartment buildings designed as blocks perpendicular to the street.

Controlling for these variables defined a set of streets from which twenty-one were selected according to the following criteria (Appleyard, 1976, p. 33):

1. *Traffic Volume.* A range of traffic volumes was sought from very lightly trafficked streets up to one which carried over 50,000 vehicles per day. The streets will be categorized:

Light Streets	0 to 2,000 vehicles per day
Medium Streets	2,000 to 10,000 vehicles per day
Heavy Streets	10,000 to 20,000 vehicles per day
Very Heavy Streets	over 20,000 vehicles per day

This follows the classification of the Street Livability Study.

2. *Paired Streets.* The original intention was to interview on streets parallel and perpendicular to main streets in order to determine the indirect or neighborhood effect of traffic. We were reduced to considering parallel streets due to budget limitations.

3. *One-way/Two-way.* We wished to make comparisons between one- and two-way streets in the morning and evening peak hours.

4. *Trees and Landscaping.* Some streets were selected to study the ameliorative effects of planting on heavier trafficked streets.

    A range of income groups was to be interviewed within each traffic volume category to determine any differences in response due to income under similar traffic conditions.

Six light streets, five medium streets, seven heavy streets, and three very heavy streets (one of which contained two study sites) were selected for the final sample (see Table 5-3). A total of 428 randomly selected in-house interviews were conducted at the twenty-two study sites. Fixty-six percent of the sample were either professionals or white-collar workers; twenty-one percent were blue-collar workers; four percent were unskilled; and nineteen percent were students, retired, or unemployed.

The issues explored in the interviews included satisfaction with the street, street images, environmental and social priorities, what bothers most, annoyance, aspects of street life, and perceptions of traffic. Table 5-4 presents a sampling of the kinds of items or concerns that related to the different issues.

The items are derived both from open-ended questions in which the respondents provided the items—for example, when asked what bothered them most —and from fixed-response questions in which the interviewer provided the items —for example, by asking respondents to rate street maintenance from "very well kept up" to "not at all kept up."

The findings from this study tended to support most of the hypotheses of the first study. In general, residents' satisfaction with and evaluation of their streets declined as traffic increased. Safety problems, noise, and air pollution were perceived to increase with traffic volume. There appeared to be a threshold effect at about 10,000 vehicles per day, however, after which the perceived problems seemed to level off. Severe parking, maintenance, and crime problems were noted on medium streets where there were fewer families (see Table 5-3). Light streets were found to be more pleasant, but residents expressed fear for children's safety, probably because children play in these streets. Finally, traffic-related problems, headed by danger and noise, were perceived to be the most severe street problems.

Streets in the Mission District

The third study, an extension of the second, was intended to identify the effects of traffic on an inner-city neighborhood of relatively low-income Latin Americans. Data from four streets, selected from the sample of 22, were analyzed to obtain greater insight into variation in the responses. The streets selected were Shotwell (light, 566 VPD), Folsom (medium, 8,319 VPD), South Van Ness (heavy, 12,771 VPD) and Army Street (very heavy, 27,284 VPD) (see Table 5-3).

In contrast with the general findings based on data from all streets, residents' satisfaction on these selected streets increased with increased traffic volume. It is important to note, however, that income was also higher on the heavier volume streets. The presence of a violent youth group on the medium and heavy streets tended to somewhat overshadow traffic concerns. The light street, which was perceived as safest for children, was also very heavily populated with children. This street, the poorest, was also the dirtiest. Overall, the anxiety over traffic expressed by the residents of these streets in the Mission District was much higher than for other streets.

LEARNING FROM THE CASE STUDIES

The two cases presented in this chapter differ in significant ways, even though they both represent evaluations of existing environments. These differences are explored in the following pages, using the evaluation schema intro-

Table 5-3. Characteristics of Selected Streets

	Traffic Volume	Peak Volume	Mean Speed	Road Width	Effve. Width	Moving Lanes	Dwelling Types			Setback & Sidewalk	Median Income
							Single Family	Duplex	Apt./ Other		
Beaumont	210	25	20–25	28	14	2	30	70	—	25	19,474
Juanita	415	51	20–25	22	10	2	100	—	—	17	18,075
Magellan	557	74	20–25	28	14	2	100	—	20	26	23,879
Shotwell	566	52	20	14	2	—	—	80	—	24	6,495
Hearst	639	63	25	28	14	2	90	10	—	18	9,150
18th Ave.	1,894	176	30–35	38	24	2	70	30	—	23	12,600
6th Ave.	5,475	503	25–30	38	24	2	50	50	—	16	10,775
Sacramento	6,298	604	25	38	24	4	—	50	40	16	14,525
Folsom	8,319	905	30–35	46	32	4	—	80	20	25	8,020
Stanyan	9,278	818	25–30	42	28	4	50	40	10	16	12,385
Dolores	9,923	984	30–35	62	48	4	10	90	—	20	10,190
S. Van Ness	12,771	1,298	30–35	46	32	4	40	10	50	13	9,610
7th Ave.	13,865	1,343	25–30	38	24	3	40	40	20	12	13,175
Pine	14,088	1,699	30	62	48	3	50	40	10	18	17,090
Monterey	14,523	1,232	35–40	50	36	4	50	30	20	13	14,725
Bush	15,313	1,448	30	62	48	3	30	40	30	25	10,275
Dewey	15,415	1,390	30	46	32	4	100	—	—	26	16,740
California	18,683	1,491	30–35	62	48	4	11	78	11	12	15,680
Portola	23,974	2,243	35–40	50	36	4	100	—	—	27	13,275
Army (project)	27,284	2,451	35–40	56	42	6	60	40	—	—	3,815
Army (street)	27,284	2,451	35–40	56	42	6	60	40	—	10	11,590
19th Ave.	52,275	3,882	30	110	96	6	70	20	10	12	11,205

Table 5-3, continued. Characteristics of Selected Streets

	Traffic Volume	Peak Volume	Mean Speed	Ethnicity				Family Composition			
				Black	Latin	Oriental	White	Under 5	5–9	10–14	Over 65
Beaumont	210	25	20–25	—	—	12	88	10	—	5	60
Juanita	415	51	20–25	—	—	6	94	15	15	15	20
Magellan	557	74	20–25	—	—	—	100	25	25	20	25
Shotwell	566	52	20	—	67	6	28	15	15	25	40
Hearst	639	63	25	—	21	7	71	10	20	20	50
18th Ave.	1,894	176	30–35	—	6	6	88	25	—	10	40
6th Ave.	5,475	503	25–30	—	—	10	90	10	—	10	20
Sacramento	6,298	604	25	23	—	—	77	5	—	5	15
Folsom	8,319	905	30–35	19	31	6	44	35	40	15	—
Stanyan	9,278	818	25–30	—	—	9	91	5	—	5	55
Dolores	9,923	984	30–35	—	30	—	70	—	—	5	10
S. Van Ness	12,771	1,298	30–35	—	23	6	71	10	25	5	40
7th Ave.	13,865	1,343	25–30	—	11	33	55	5	10	10	20
Pine	14,088	1,699	30	50	17	—	50	15	20	15	15
Monterey	14,523	1,232	35–40	8	—	—	75	10	20	5	15
Bush	15,313	1,448	30	69	—	—	31	—	—	5	10
Dewey	15,415	1,390	30	—	—	10	90	20	—	5	20
California	18,683	1,491	30–35	41	6	12	41	5	15	15	5
Portola	23,974	2,243	35–40	—	—	5	95	20	5	5	55
Army (project)	27,284	2,451	35–40	64	18	—	18	60	20	33	—
Army (street)	27,284	2,451	35–40	—	57	—	43	15	15	31	15
19th Ave.	52,275	3,882	30	—	5	26	69	—	5	5	50

From Liveable Urban Streets: Managing Auto Traffic in Neighborhoods, by D. Appleyard. Washington, D.C.: U.S. Government Printing Office, 1976.

Table 5-4. Selected Interview Issues and Items

Issue	*Selected Items or Concerns*
Satisfaction with the street	Original expectations Comparisons with other streets Good for children Preferences for a busy or quiet street
Street images	Appearance Cleanliness Friendliness Noise
Environmental and social priorities	Cleanliness Security from crime Attractive appearance Greenery Access: parks, shops, work, downtown
What bothers most	Traffic Noise Appearance
Annoyance	Traffic danger Dangerous vehicles (trucks, buses) Pollution (noise, air) Appearance/maintenance Inconvenience Crime Adaptive behavior (close windows, keep children off street)
Aspects of street life	Safety: traffic versus crime Noise and air pollution Privacy and territory Feelings of home Friends and neighbors Activities on street Strangers Appearance and maintenance
Perceptions of traffic	Awareness Perceived volume and speed When traffic is heaviest One-way or two-way Preferred improvements

From *Liveable Urban Streets: Managing Auto Traffic in Neighborhoods,* by D. Appleyard. Washington, D.C.: U.S. Government Printing Office, 1976.

duced in Chapter 1 as a structuring device for the comparative analysis and discussion.

The Institutional Dimension

The coastal zone and the city streets studies were undertaken for different reasons. The coastal zone study was undertaken to provide information on the quality of the existing environment, on existing problems or needs, and for the development of specific planning recommendations for specific places. The city streets study was intended as a basis for the development of conceptual models for understanding the effects of traffic on residential neighborhoods. Thus, the coastal zone study was undertaken with a specific set of decision-makers in mind, the executive and legislative branches of the Virgin Islands government. Recommendations were prepared by the planning office (a part of the Governor's Office) to be acted on by the Virgin Islands Senate. The city streets study was addressed to transportation and planning officials in cities across the country.

The coastal zone study was undertaken as part of the planning program and was designed by the Virgin Islands Planning Office staff and their consultants. The city streets study was financed by the Federal Highway Administration and was conducted at the University of California, Berkeley, by faculty and students from the College of Environmental Design.

As indicated previously, both studies are responsive to existing public policy. The coastal-zone study relates directly to the mandates of the Coastal Zone Management Act of 1972. The city-streets study, however, does not have such a specific tie but rather relates in a more general way to a number of legislative policies enacted between 1937 and 1977.

The following example illustrates one way in which survey data were fed into the coastal zone management program. The survey found that there was high agreement among groups and islands in regard to the need to protect certain areas from development, and on the identification of the most scenic areas. This finding supported the drafting of a policy statement to:

> protect and enhance the characteristics of those shoretypes which are most valued by the public as amenities and which are scarce, which will be significantly altered in character by development, or which will cause significant environmental degradations if developed, and to direct growth to shoretypes of "lower value" which are abundant and less vulnerable to damage. (Virgin Islands Planning Office 1977b: p. 91.)

This policy was expressed in the land and water use plan by identifying and limiting the range of possible uses of highly valued scenic areas and of areas perceived as meriting protection under the plan. For example, present practices of removing mangrove vegetation indiscriminately to accommodate commercial and recreational (boating) activities would be curtailed and passive recreational and conservation uses only would be permitted.

The identification of potential conflicts between professional judgments and residents' perceptions, as indicated previously with regard to salt ponds, is another example of the potential utility of the survey data. These data help to define areas and issues in which decision-makers may elect to follow professional judgments rather than user perceptions, and in which educational programs may be required if environmentally based planning objectives are to be successfully implemented.

The data also suggest areas in which the value orientations of professional planners may differ from those for whom the planning is being done. For example, members of the planning staff undertook detailed analyses of the visual character (kind and extent of development) and aesthetic qualities of beaches. These data were prepared as general planning background information. The professionals consistently ranked undeveloped beaches more scenic than developed beaches. This is a value orientation shared by many continentals, but apparently not by Virgin Islanders (for example, see: Wohlwill, 1976; Zube, 1976). The participants in the survey did not consistently place a higher scenic value on undeveloped beaches than on developed beaches. Thus, proposals and policies relating to the potential preservation of some undeveloped beaches could not be supported with the argument that they were also more beautiful. Instead, the rationale and justification would have to be based more on the kinds of experiences and activities more readily available at an undeveloped beach, or, perhaps, on the desirability of maintaining some options for beach use open for the future.

Potential uses for the data and findings from the city streets study are less precisely defined because of the more general focus on the evaluation. Nevertheless, a number of possible uses are apparent, including use for predicting consequences of implementing alternative traffic-management plans, such as changing to one-way streets or redirecting through traffic away from residential areas.

The Environmental Dimension

The development of predictive models usually includes a search for physical correlates of perceptual/experiential responses. The notion is that if measurable physical attributes or characteristics of a specific domain can be identified that co-vary with user responses in systematic and reliable ways, those same attributes or characteristics can be used as indicators or predictors of the quality of proposed future environments. Assessments of the quality of existing environments, therefore, provide an important component of the data base for developing such predictive models. The city streets study includes the essential user-response and physical-attribute elements.

The domains of both studies are clearly identified as coastal zone and city streets. The kinds of physical attributes used to define and sub-divide the domains differ considerably, however. As indicated in Table 5-3, the city streets study included attributes such as traffic volume, speed, and width. These are attributes that, theoretically, are susceptible to manipulation if reliable associations with users' perceptual responses are found to exist.

The coastal zone study used a biophysical subdivision of the domain. This kind of sub-division, or taxonomy, was used, primarily, in order to be able to relate the household survey data as directly as possible to a natural resources inventory that was an essential ingredient of the planning program and used the same taxonomy.

There is an important difference between the two studies in the standards, criteria, and measurement systems used. Both studies used household surveys. The city streets study elicited user responses only to their own streets. It tended to be more person-centered and resulted in personal, subjective responses. The coastal zone study was place-centered and elicited comparative appraisals of the various coastal environments depicted on the displays used in the interviews. In other words, the coastal zone survey provided respondents with an array of settings to evaluate comparatively. The qualitative range was defined in large part by the depicted coastal environments. Respondents in the city street study were asked to attend primarily to their perceptions of and experiences on the street in which they lived.

The two studies involved different ways of representing the environment to respondents. In the city streets study participants were interviewed in situ, much as would be the case with an evaluation of a neighborhood or housing project. In the other study, however, respondents were presented with color photographs (simulations) of the environment. They were not necessarily in the midst of the areas being evaluated while participating in a perceptual/experiential-based evaluative task. This raises the obvious question of the validity of using photographic surrogates for "real-world" experience. A number of studies have investigated this question (Coughlin & Goldstein, 1970; Zube, Pitt & Anderson, 1974; Daniel & Boster, 1976).

The data from these inquiries are convincing, and indicate consistently high correlations between on-site aesthetic evaluations and aesthetic evaluations based on photographs of the sites. All of the studies involved rural and natural landscape settings only. Whether or not similarly convincing findings would obtain for the use of photographic simulations for urban settings or for other than aesthetic evaluations, however, is an open question at this time (see Chapter 6 for additional discussion on simulation).

The use of photographic simulations in the Virgin Islands study also raises a question about how the photographs are to be selected—that is, how the environment is to be sampled. This is an important and common question in evaluation studies of large areas for planning inventories. The stratified sample in this study used representative examples from each of the coastal environments. Other sampling procedures that have been used for evaluation studies include random sampling (Daniel & Boster, 1976), cross-sectional sampling (Zube, Pitt & Anderson, 1974), and opportunity sampling (Shafer & Mietz, 1969). Random sampling is usually the ideal procedure, because it minimizes the possibility of biasing the sample and, therefore, enhances the validity of findings. In many landscapes, however, it is virtually impossible to gain access to and obtain photographs of selected geographic locations. Natural barriers such as topography, water, and private property boundaries can preclude reasonable access to and mobility over the landscape, or make the cost of obtaining the sample prohibitive.

Cross-sectional sampling offers an alternative procedure whereby photographs are obtained at predetermined points along a transect—for example, along a roadway—that traverses the study landscape. In the absence of an existing pathway of some sort, cross-sectional sampling can encounter the same access and mobility problems as random sampling.

Opportunity samples are probably most common, and frequently used when physical and economic constraints are encountered. Opportunity samples are, in effect, available samples—for example, selections from an existing collection of photographs. They are the weakest form of sampling. Nevertheless, when other forms of samples cannot be obtained, they can be used with reasonable ease and with caution in the analysis and interpretation of data.

The Participatory Dimension

Both studies identified individual and group characteristics, but tended to emphasize the latter. Ethnicity, income, and age were important characteristics in the city street study. Native/continental (place of origin or length of residence), education, and island of residence were important characteristics in the coastal zone study. In both cases, these characteristics were used primarily as a means of analyzing potential differences among groups.

The coastal zone planning activity employed multiple-participation modes to provide opportunity for interaction. Public hearings on each of the islands, along with a technical committee and planning workshops with special interest groups, were used to foster interaction between planners and others. The city street study, however, was not intended to provide opportunity for interaction of users with the planning process as it was not a part of a planning activity aimed at the modification of a specific environment.

Both of the studies employed random sampling procedures to identify participants. The Virgin Islands study, however, followed a geographically stratified, random-sampling procedure to ensure minimum-sized samples in each of the sub-areas used for planning purposes. As noted previously, in our discussion on the sampling of environments, random sampling is the desired procedure, since bias in selecting participants is minimized and the validity of findings is enhanced. The issue of sampling users or participants is discussed again in Chapter 8, noting some of the differences encountered in the case studies in this chapter and in Chapters 6 and 7.

CHAPTER EXERCISE

Imagine that your hometown is undertaking an inventory of existing open spaces (parks, playgrounds and plazas) as a preliminary step in revising and updating their open-space plan. They already have a quantitative inventory that includes specific locations and sizes of open spaces and the developed facilities at each site. What is needed at this time is a qualitative inventory. What are the public's perceptions of the quality of the open spaces?

If your home is in a large city, consider just one sector of the city. What are some of the important issues to be considered in the design of such an inventory? How would you select the residents to participate in the study? For example, what are the advantages and disadvantages of using random sampling of house-holds versus random sampling of users in the spaces being evaluated? What would you do to ensure a higher probability that the data obtained would be useful for the subsequent plan development?

Prepare a report, in the form of a proposal, to the city planning department, setting forth in some detail the study you would propose. If the planning department responded enthusiastically to your proposal, but asked you:

1. to do it in three months rather than the nine that you proposed, or
2. to reduce the scope of your study because of funding limitations,

how would you respond? Are there alternative ways of implementing the study? Could the study be reduced in scope? How might those decisions affect data utility and reliability?

SUPPLEMENTARY READINGS

The Quality of American Life presents a detailed report on a national survey of Americans' satisfaction with their physical, social, and institutional environ-ment, and their perceptions of the quality of life. In contrast with the inventory case studies in this chapter, this report does not address specific places. It provides data representative of the national adult (over 18) population.

Campbell, A., Converse, P. E., and Rogers, W. L. *The quality of American life.* New York: Russell Sage Foundation, 1976.

The Quality of Nonmetropolitan Living provides a similar report in a specific geographic area. It looks at residents' evaluations of the environments and their attitudes toward an array of environmental issues in a popular recreation area in the state of Michigan.

Marans, R. W., and Wellman, J. D. *The quality of nonmetropolitan living: Evaluations, behaviors and expectations of Northern Michigan residents.* Ann Arbor: Institute for Social Research, University of Michigan, 1978.

Chapter 6

EVALUATING
ALTERNATIVE FUTURES

A NEW SET OF PROBLEMS

Who are the users of future environments, and how are they informed about the nature of these environments? For example, what will the environment look like, what opportunities will be provided for physical activities and social interactions, what will be the distribution of spaces, and what materials, colors, and textures will be used?

The question of who the users are and of who participates in the evaluation becomes more difficult to answer as the time span between the proposal for a change and the implementation of the change becomes greater. Individuals who participate in the evaluation of alternative designs for a new neighborhood park may no longer be living in the neighborhood by the time it is built. It is not uncommon for four or five years to elapse while waiting for the city to approve a tax increase or bond issue to pay for the park, followed by another year or more of waiting for the land to be cleared and the park to be built. In general, the larger the project, the longer it takes for approval and implementation and, hence, the more difficult it is to identify the actual users.

To inform participants about the nature of the future environment, it must be simulated in some way. The traditional land-use maps and construction drawings prepared by planners and designers represent one form of simulation. Frequently, however, these maps and drawings are highly technical and consist of symbols or abstractions most readily understood by other professionals. Planners and designers also use perspective sketches, drawings of building elevations, and three-dimensional models to communicate the nature of proposed projects. These are all forms of static simulations—graphic representations of future three-dimensional environments. They are intended to provide as much information as possible about the shapes, sizes, colors, textures, and materials of the future environment.

Dynamic simulations (see Figure 6-1) consist of "the provision of an infinite variety of continuously variable concrete 'views' of a place" (McKechnie, 1977, p. 173). For example, dynamic simulations are created by making movies of three-dimensional models. Simulated eye-level walks or drives can be created

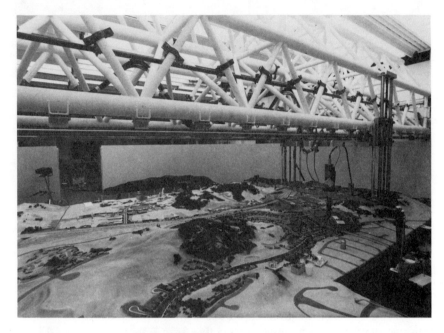

Figure 6-1. Photograph of the Berkeley environmental simulator. (Photo courtesy of Donald Appleyard and Kenneth H. Craik.)

by moving the camera through the model along a simulated walkway or road. Speed, elevation above ground, and eye movement from right to left can all be simulated to enhance the apparent validity of the experience.

Three case studies are presented in this chapter. Two employed three-dimensional model simulations. The third used architectural drawings. In both of the cases using models, participants responded to photos of the models rather than to the models themselves. The models also differed considerably in the amount of detail portrayed and in their visual approximation of real forms and materials.

MANAGING NIAGARA FALLS

From 1965 to 1970, several congressional and administrative actions were initiated, and an international study undertaken to investigate enhancement of the scenic beauty and aspects of public safety at the American Falls at Niagara (American Falls International Board, 1974). These actions and the study were precipitated by several rockfalls over the past forty years, with more anticipated in the future, indicating that the Falls were in a significant stage of change. The three largest rockfalls from the crest occurred in 1931 (35,000 cubic yards), July 1954 (83,000 cubic yards), and December 1954 (10,000 cubic yards).

The effects of these rockfalls included an increase in the amount of talus (accumulated rock) at the base of the Falls, and a reduction in the free fall of the water from the crest to the base. Geological studies indicated the possibility of potentially dangerous additional falls in areas adjacent to viewing points. Four such rockfalls near viewing points have caused serious injury or death to nine people since 1907.

The Falls

Niagara Falls (see Figure 6-2) is a scenic resource known and recognized around the world. It attracts ten million visitors annually. The Falls are the result of the continual natural process of erosion. They have retreated over a period of approximately 12,000 years, creating a gorge approximately seven miles long. Management of both the American and the Canadian Falls, particularly in reference to the amount of water that can be withdrawn upstream for power generation, is governed by international treaties.

The International Joint Commission has long been concerned with the aesthetic qualities of the Falls. Parks have been established on both the American and Canadian sides. The area surrounding the Falls and parks, however, has been a subject of frequent criticism for its honky-tonk, neon garishness.

Figure 6-2. Aerial view of the American Falls at Niagara, New York.

The Study

The study of the American Falls encompassed technical components on geology, rock mechanics, hydrology, and engineering, and design components on landscape architecture and aesthetics. Recognizing the inevitable public interest in the study, several methods were used to keep the public informed and to elicit public response, including news releases, press conferences, displays, exhibits, pamphlets, public hearings, a seminar of professional experts, and a questionnaire. The primary issues finally addressed in the study were:

> "Should man intervene in the natural process of so vast a phenomenon for either aesthetic or safety reasons? How important is the relationship between this natural spectacle and the man-made environment—the immediate surroundings and the larger regional environment?" (American Falls International Board, 1974, p. 2.)

Three possible alternatives for aesthetic enhancement were considered: (1) removal of most of the fallen rock at the base of the Falls; (2) raising the water level of the Maid of the Mist Pool at the base of the Falls to its former level, thereby covering some of the fallen rock; and (3) increasing the flow of water over the American Falls. To facilitate the conceptualization of these alternatives a hydrological model was constructed at a scale of one-fiftieth of the actual size of the Falls. The model was approximately twenty-two feet long and four feet high. It was constructed so that varying amounts of talus could be removed, flow over the crest could be varied, and the pool level raised and lowered.

The first public hearing was held in 1966, the second in 1967, and the third and final hearing in 1972. Table 6-1 presents a summary of the primary agenda items, and the general outcome from each hearing. It is not clear how many individuals participated in the second and third hearings, but they may have attracted a few more than the first. Overall, the attendance was not very impressive.

A seminar held in June 1972 was made up of a group of fifteen environmental planners and landscape architects from the United States and Canada. Participants were asked to consider the three alternatives for enhancing the aesthetics of the Falls. With remarkable unanimity, the participants took a broader view of the issues and expanded the area of interest to include the environment surrounding the Falls. Their recommendations (American Falls International Board, 1974, p. F14) included:

1. Funds that might be used for talus removal might better be spent to purchase land to guard against further intrusions on the view of the Falls.
2. A comprehensive transportation system, excluding cars, should be developed, making it easy for all, including handicapped, to view the Falls.
3. An environmental interpretive or educational system should be developed.
4. An urban design review committee should be established to look at intrusions on the view.
5. Management of the Niagara Falls *area* should be done by an International Body.

Table 6-1. Summary of Public Hearings

Hearings	Attendance	Agenda	General Outcome
January 18, 1966, conducted by the Buffalo District Corps of Engineers in City Hall, Niagara Falls, New York.	Ninety-nine individuals including representatives from many organizations, and the Mayor of Niagara Falls.	1. Should work be done to preserve and enhance the scenic beauty of the American Falls? 2. What is the scope of work desired? 3. What agency or agencies would participate in the work and cost?	Participants were in favor of a study being undertaken.
October 24, 1967, conducted by the International Joint Commission in Niagara Falls, New York. October 25, 1967, held in Niagara Falls, Ontario.	Transcripts do not indicate the exact number.	The general purpose of the hearing was to inquire into the matter of the preservation of the American Falls, to obtain suggestions on how this should be done, and to hear any comments by the American Falls International Board that was appointed by the Commission.	Virtually all the witnesses stated or implied that they were in favor of steps being taken to preserve and restore the beauty of the American Falls. The Commission announced they would request that the two Governments take the necessary steps to construct a temporary cofferdam for the purpose of dewatering the American Falls. The prospect of a temporary dewatering of the American Falls was viewed by a number of those who gave testimony as a potential and unique tourist attraction.
March 24, 1972, conducted by the International Joint Commission in City Hall, Niagara Falls, New York.	Transcripts do not indicate the exact number.	This hearing was pursuant to the American Falls International Board report, dated December 1971.	Records indicate the participants were in favor of a study being undertaken. Suggestions for topics to be considered throughout the remainder of the study included: 1. The undesirability of dewatering during seasons of freeze and thaw. 2. The possible abandonment of the Ontario Power Plant. 3. The winter scene as a reason for leaving the talus as it is. 4. The aesthetic aspects of pollution. 5. The possibility of increasing the flow over the American Falls.

Figure 6-3. Model of the Falls as they exist without any fallen rock removed.

To expand opportunities for the public to contribute to the decision-making process, a twelve-page brochure was published illustrating the three alternatives, with photos of the hydrological model and the actual Falls. Figures 6-3, 6-4, and 6-5 illustrate the model and two of the alternatives. A detachable postcard-sized questionnaire was included with the brochure asking for responses to the three alternatives. The brochure also provided estimated cost information for the implementation of the alternatives: talus removal, one to ten million dollars; increased flow, six million dollars; and raising the pool level, 8.7 million dollars. The brochure made no mention, however, of the natural history of the Falls and the process of erosion the Falls exemplify. Two hundred thousand copies were printed in English for both Canada and the United States (100,000 each), and 20,000 were printed in French.

Figure 6-4. Model of the Falls showing removal of most of the fallen rock at the base.

Figure 6-5. Model of the Falls showing the restored level of the Maid of the Mist Pool and covering about one-third of the accumulated rock.

Three educational publications directed at elementary- and high-school students also carried stories based on the brochure and provided copies of the postcard questionnaire (*Current Events, Current Science,* and *Scholastic News Trail*). On September 9, 1973 the *New York Times* carried a nine-page feature article on the study, including a reproduction of the questionnaire. In contrast to the brochure and the *Current Science* articles, which were somewhat biased toward making a change, the *New York Times* article emphasized the process of erosion and the surrounding honky-tonk environment, and was biased toward making no change.

Over 75,000 responses were received. Response to the brochure and to the *Current Science* article reflected the biased presentations, and favored one or more of the alternatives by margins of two-to-one and four-to-one, respectively. The thousands of responses to the *New York Times* article, however, were overwhelmingly in favor of making no change. Responses to other sources were about equally divided between change and no change. Many of the free-response comments, made in space provided on the questionnaire, were directed to the appearance of the surrounding environment.

Mixed Results

Public participation in this planning process spanned eight years, from the first public hearing in 1966 to the questionnaire response, which continued until 1974. During this period of time, the swing of the pendulum went from predominantly supportive of change to a significant evidence of negative response to change—most strongly stated by the seminar group of professionals. There was, nevertheless, considerable agreement among the later respondents about concern for the surrounding environment and a stronger conservation-oriented outlook on the Falls.

The American Falls International Board, which had responsibility for the study, concluded that the qualitative questions

". . . do not demand an immediate decision and that those answers should be made only after the greater environmental questions have been studied. Further, the Board concludes that the guiding policy should be to accept the process of change as a dynamic part of the natural condition of the Falls and that the process of erosion and recession should not be interrupted, and this policy is consistent with the public and experts' conservationist outlook" (American Falls International Board, 1974, p. F17).

DESIGNS FOR A CITY PARK

During the winter of 1975–1976, the Parks and Recreation Department of Ann Arbor, Michigan was in the process of developing plans for the construction of a new city park. Landscape architects Terry Brown and Charles Cares were commissioned to design the park on a plot of land located in downtown Ann Arbor (see Figure 6-6).

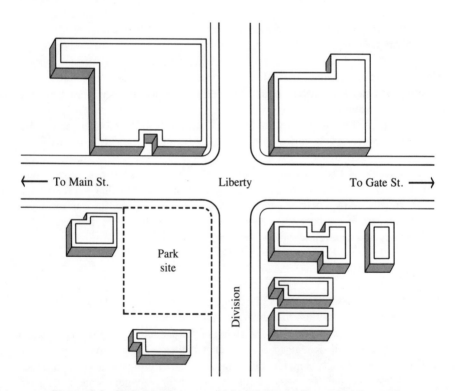

Figure 6-6. Park location map. (Adapted from *Liberty Division Park: Citizen Survey,* by R. Kaplan. Report to the Ann Arbor Parks and Recreation Department, Michigan, January 1976. Used by permission.)

Alternative Designs

Three alternatives for the design of the park were proposed by the landscape architects. The designs varied in the way walls, benches, and trees were used to create different seating arrangements and distributions of open and tree-covered spaces. One alternative also included a large-scale, abstract sculpture.

Simple models were constructed of each of the alternatives. Model-scale people and cars were included to convey information about the relative size of the trees in the park and of the surrounding buildings. Relatively little detail was shown on the surrounding buildings.

Eight photographs of each model were selected to represent the various views and attributes of the proposed park. For the alternative that included the sculpture, six of the eight photographs included the sculpture in the view—in some as a focal feature, and in some as part of the general park setting.

Evaluating the Alternatives

Environmental psychologist Rachel Kaplan (1976) was asked by the Superintendent of the Parks and Recreation Department to conduct a study of citizen responses to the alternative designs. She developed a survey that focused on components or characteristics of the alternatives rather than on the individual designs. In other words, the evaluation sought to identify which elements or characteristics of all alternatives were most preferred by citizens, rather than which was the preferred alternative.

Eight photographs of each of these alternatives were mounted on 11 inch by 13 inch boards. Four boards were prepared with each board containing two photographs of each alternative.

Participants were asked to respond to each photograph on a five-point rating scale (1 = not at all . . . 5 = a great deal) in terms of "how much you like it? How pleasing would you find it if the park was like that?" Opportunity was also provided for participants to offer comments in writing on the response form, or verbally to an interviewer who recorded these responses.

Background information collected on participants included age, sex, job/student status, and whether they lived or worked in downtown Ann Arbor.

Who Participated

Participation in the study was voluntary. However, prior to the study, a letter signed by the Superintendent of Parks and Recreation was sent to all residents and businesspersons in the area of the proposed park. The letter briefly described the study and invited everyone to participate. The two locations where the study was to be conducted were identified (a local bank and the public library), as were the scheduled days and hours. Employees and others who happened to be at the two study locations but who had not received the letter were also able to participate.

In all, 181 people completed the evaluation. The sample was nearly evenly divided between the two locations, on the basis of sex, and in terms of people who lived and/or worked downtown and those who neither lived nor worked there.

Patterns of Preference

Kaplan employed an analytical tool that grouped or clustered the patterns of similarities among the ratings of the individual photographs (see R. Kaplan, 1972). Groups of pictures were identified for which participants responded in similar ways and for which salient components or design characteristics could be identified. Five clusters of photographs were identified as indicated in Table 6-2. An example from each cluster is depicted in Figures 6-7 through 6-11. The preference patterns or park elements and characteristics evaluated most highly are quite evident in Table 6-2. The sculpture was obviously not strongly endorsed by participants. On the other hand, generous tree plantings and ample opportunities for sitting were highly desired elements and characteristics.

The difference in ratings among sub-groups defined on the basis of age, sex, or job/student status were negligible. An interesting difference did emerge, however, between those who only worked downtown and those who lived downtown or lived and worked downtown. The former group ranked the sitting in the park cluster significantly higher and, in fact, ranked it the highest of any cluster by any sub-group. Kaplan suggests that this may be attributable to differing perceptions of these sub-groups with respect to the safety and pleasantness of daytime use by workers and the potential after-dark threat to those who live there.

Table 6-2. Photograph Groupings

Grouping	No. of Photos in Group	Mean Rating for All Photos in Group
Sculpture	6	2.57
Tree canopy, low emphasis on sitting	3	2.83
Relatively open, with a tree-covered portion	7	2.98
Sitting in the park amongst the trees	4	3.11
Built emphasis, low walls, benches, and variety of trees	4	3.14

From *Liberty Division Park: Citizen Survey,* by R. Kaplan. Report to the Ann Arbor Parks and Recreation Department, Michigan, January 1976. Used by permission.

Figure 6-7. Sculpture cluster. (Figures 6-7 through 6-11 from *Liberty Division Park: Citizen Survey*, by R. Kaplan. Report to the Ann Arbor Parks and Recreation Department, Michigan, January 1976. Used by permission.)

Figure 6-8. Tree canopy: low-emphasis or sitting cluster.

Figure 6-9. Relatively open cluster.

Parks can provide environments for muggers at night in places that would appear in the daytime to be composed of pleasant plantings and secluded sitting places.

Free-response comments, of which there were many, tended to support and reinforce the preference patterns identified in the clusters. The sculpture received its share of comments—ranging from strongly negative to strongly positive. Areas of strong agreement among respondents included "anti-concrete" feelings; endorsement of green growing things; and the importance of seating, and a sense of spaciousness.

SELECTING BUILDING FORMS

Buildings are complex systems of spaces, materials, mechanical and structural components, forms, colors, and textures that are intended to accommodate and support specific human functions and activities. Many architects have traditionally attempted to design the exterior of buildings so that they convey a message to users about the functions housed within, and about the general character of the interior. In our vocabulary we refer to some buildings as uninviting and austere, and others as warm and inviting. Also, there are building designs that become stereotyped and are known as shopping-center, industrial, or institutional architecture.

The initial visual impression can certainly influence future users' perceptions of the buildings they are going to use for living, working, studying, or playing. Visual impressions contribute to our expectations of satisfaction or dissatisfaction with these environments.

Figure 6-10. Sitting-in-the-park cluster.

Options for the Client and the Architect

Ewing Miller of Archonics Corporation of Indianapolis, Indiana, a firm of architects, planners, and engineers, has had a long history of working with psychologist Lawrence Wheeler and using applied behavioral-science methods as a means of arriving at more informed planning and design decisions. Early in the

Figure 6-11. Built-emphasis cluster.

Figure 6-12. Too corporate, not inviting. (Figures 6-12 through 6-15: photos courtesy of Ewing Miller, Archonics Corporation.)

development of each project, usually after completion of the design program and the development of conceptual plans (see Figure 4-2), they prepare a series of options, or alternatives, for the client's consideration.

There are several reasons for the development of the options at this stage. First, it provides an early opportunity for the client to participate directly in the design. Second, it gives the architect an opportunity to use the options as an educational tool, informing the client as to what is possible and how the building's forms and massing are responsive to the program—that is, to the client's needs and wants. And, third, it gives both the client and the architect an opportunity to explore the meanings that each derives from the several options.

Figures 6-12 and 6-13 depict two of several design alternatives presented to members of an Ohio laborers' organization for their proposed training and recreation center. The basic difference in the alternatives is the treatment of the roof. Figure 6-12, which was rejected by the members, was perceived as "too corporate," like "Exxon." The strong horizontal line and large overhang for solar control, while viewed as more masculine, was perceived as less inviting and not expressive of the lodge or resort atmosphere that was thought desirable in order to encourage attendance for learning. The accepted alternative, Figure 6-13, was

Figure 6-13. Less formal—more like a private club.

Figure 6-14. Reminiscent of houses or a small settlement.

perceived as less formal and more like a private club. The decision, arrived at in meetings of the membership, was based on image, pride, and suggested symbolism.

Two alternatives for the exterior of an elementary school in Indiana are shown in Figures 6-14 and 6-15. The children who would attend this school, and their parents, participated in the discussion of the alternatives and the selection of the one with the most satisfying and pleasing form and massing. Both alternatives were liked, but Figure 6-14 was accepted because the clustered arrangement and pitched roofs were reminiscent of houses or a small settlement. Figure 6-15 was viewed by the children and their parents as suggestive of a civic center, or of shopping-center architecture.

LEARNING FROM THE CASE STUDIES

The evaluation of alternative futures, as suggested previously, can present problems not usually encountered in the evaluation of existing environments. Among these are the identification of the users and the need to accurately portray or describe future environments. Like inventory evaluations, however, alternative futures evaluations are almost always undertaken for a specific client.

Figure 6-15. Suggestive of a civic center or a shopping center.

The Institutional Dimension

In each of the cases discussed in this chapter, the evaluation process was viewed as an important and significant means of facilitating citizen participation. The studies were undertaken and funded as an integral part of the design process. Both the City Park and the Building Form studies had direct effects on the final designs that were constructed. Specific attributes or characteristics preferred by potential users were identified and used by the designers in the preparation of final plans for construction. The findings of the Niagara Falls study provided one set of data to be considered by the International Joint Commission in their deliberations, along with the findings from the public hearings and the professional seminar. Unfortunately, the contrasting biases in the brochure and in the newspaper accounts detracted from the validity of the findings. Thus, their utility as a dominant factor influencing the Commission's decision had to be seriously questioned.

The evaluation strategy followed in each of the cases was elicitation of direct response to photographs of simulated environments. Each study also provided an opportunity for free responses in addition to structured or forced-choice responses. In each case, these free responses provided the decision-makers with a richness of information about users' perceptions that would not otherwise have been available.

The Building Form and Niagara Falls studies were primarily responsive to aesthetic goals and objectives. The City Park study, however, addressed the goal of user-satisfaction, as well as aesthetics. Opportunities and modes of use of the park were important issues in the evaluation of design alternatives, as well as the aesthetic effects of various components and characteristics of the designs.

The Environmental Dimension

City parks and elementary schools represent general and widely recognized environmental domains. In contrast, Niagara Falls, while also widely recognized, represents a domain of one, a unique environment. The measurement system used in each case study was that of comparison among alternatives. Participants were not asked to evaluate the alternatives in reference to a design program that stated, for example, what the functional and aesthetic attributes of city parks or elementary schools are. Rather, they were asked to simply express their preferences. The standards and criteria they employed in this process were personal and subjective. Nevertheless, the free responses in the park study, and the architects' discussions with users about the elementary school, did begin to reveal some of the standards and criteria employed by participants—such as those concerning the residential character of building form, or "anti-concrete" sentiments expressed in relation to the park alternatives.

The Niagara Falls study provides a good example of the need to construct evaluation procedures and instruments with care, so as to not bias results. It is reasonably evident that the way in which information was presented to different groups of participants caused them to attend to different issues—that is, to invoke different standards and criteria. When structural change was presented in a favorable light, without equal discussion of a conservation-oriented management program, the former was preferred. And when conservation was emphasized, the status quo was preferred. The costs of the several alternatives were also included in the information given to participants, but it was not possible to determine if and how this information influenced participants' perceptions. A balanced presentation of the alternatives, and a more carefully designed response format, probably would have resulted in a study with greater validity and utility.

The Niagara Falls study was the only one of the three in which the varying physical attributes of the alternatives were stated explicitly. These attributes included the proposed physical changes such as talus removal, water flow, and pool level.

The use of the clustering technique in the City Park study illustrates another approach to the identification of physical attributes associated with preferred alternatives. The clustering technique provides a very useful tool for studying the patterns of responses over all of the photographs of alternatives. The photographs making up each cluster can be analyzed to identify the components, or physical attributes, associated with the various preference ratings.

Each of the studies involved the use of simulation. The simulations ranged from the very sophisticated and accurate three-dimensional model representation of Niagara Falls to the more abstract and sketch-like qualities of the three-dimensional park model and the building-form drawings. While there is convincing evidence of the validity of various simulation techniques for existing environments (Zube, Pitt, & Anderson, 1975; Daniel & Boster, 1976), there has been relatively little research on the validity and reliability of simulations of future environments or environmental change. These are important issues to be investigated (see Schomaker, 1978; Wohlwill, 1978). Both the park study and the building-form study provide important opportunities, however, to investigate such questions of validity and reliability through the conduct of post-construction evaluations.

The Participatory Dimension

The participatory dimension differs considerably among the three studies, particularly in relation to user identification. Who are the users of Niagara Falls? Can only those who have visited the Falls be considered users, or are users also those who derive vicarious pleasure from reading about the Falls in elementary school textbooks or travel guides? Obviously, the Commission considered the broader definition of users. Efforts were made to solicit responses from as many users as possible, in line with the idea of an "opportunity" or accidental sample. In other words, efforts were made to obtain as many voluntary participants as was reasonably convenient and possible without following random-sampling procedures.

A nonrandom sample was also used in the City Park study. Given the more limited geographic context, it was possible to write each resident and business in the area of the proposed park and invite them to participate. Thus, the entire population was informed of the study. A similar strategy in the Niagara Falls study would have included, at the least, all residents of the country.

The users in the two building-form studies were more easily identified, and the architect was able to include essentially the entire populations in his studies.

Subgroup responses were analyzed in both the Niagara Falls and City Park studies—including age, subgroups based on place of residence, and student/job status. In most instances, differences in response on the basis of subgroups was negligible. The Park study noted an interesting difference, however, between the perceptions of the downtown residents and the downtown workers. This is probably attributable to the broader evaluative task, which encompassed potential for personal use or activity as well as an aesthetic evaluation.

A final difference in the participatory dimension among the three studies, and one which has been alluded to previously, is the specific role of the user-evaluation in the design/decision process. The Building Form studies identified the exteriors that were subsequently constructed. The Park study did not identify a specific alternative to be built. Instead, preferred components and physical attributes of the several alternatives that were identified were then used by the designer to produce the final design for construction. And, user responses to the Niagara Falls alternative were just one part of a multiple-participation process each component of which was advisory to the Commission.

CHAPTER EXERCISES

Frequently, in the development of designs, a number of graphic displays are produced—ranging from plans and elevations to perspective sketches and study models. Using one or more existing environments for which such an array of graphic displays are available or can be readily prepared, design a study to assess the perceived spatial and aesthetic qualities of the interior, building, or open space.

For example, enlist the participation of students from another class or a dormitory or housing unit to independently evaluate the design as displayed (1) in the drawings or models, (2) in photographs of the real environment, and (3) on-site, if possible. Each student should evaluate only one of the conditions. Try to get at least 15 students for each evaluation. What methods or response measures would you use in a study such as this? How would you determine the relative validity of each simulation mode as a surrogate for the real environment?

The building form case study in this chapter provides the basis for another exercise. Design a more formal and structured evaluation of the alternatives that could also be used for evaluating the buildings after construction and initial use.

For purposes of this exercise, develop a set of assumed criteria or standards relating to the building's exterior forms and aesthetics.

SUPPLEMENTARY READINGS

The chapter by Appleyard reviews environmental simulation media used in planning and design ranging from architectural drawings—plans and perspectives, three-dimensional models, and photographic techniques—to computer graphics and verbal descriptions. Criteria are suggested for evaluating media for communication with the public. McKechnie categorizes simulation techniques as either static or dynamic, and as either perceptual or conceptual. Dynamic perceptual simulation is addressed in detail and illustrated by pictures from the Berkeley Simulation Laboratory.

Appleyard, D. Understanding professional media. In I. Altman and J. Wohlwill (Eds.), *Human behavior and environment, vol. 2.* New York: Plenum Press, 1977.
McKechnie, G. E. Simulation techniques in environmental psychology. In D. Stokols (Ed.), *Perspectives on environment and behavior theory, research and applications.* New York: Plenum Press, 1977.

Chapter 7

POSTCONSTRUCTION EVALUATION

WHICH ENVIRONMENTS SHOULD BE EVALUATED, AND WHY

Hundreds of thousands of new environments are created every year, ranging from individual rooms to neighborhoods and cities. Which ones should be evaluated, and why? What are the selection criteria?

As noted in Chapter 2, the provision of satisfactory housing has been a long-standing policy goal in the United States. Similarly, albeit more recently, the provision of open space in the form of public parks and recreation areas, and accessibility through highway, street, and public transit programs, have been other policy goals. Millions of dollars have been spent in pursuit of these environmental goals without benefit of systematic evaluation of the success of the resulting environments—success as determined by the satisfaction of the users. Domains that are the result of large investments of public funds and that affect the lives of thousands of people should certainly be sampled and evaluated. These domains include publicly funded projects such as parks, subways, and housing, and privately funded projects such as shopping centers and malls. Evaluating all such environments after construction would be an enormous, costly, and inefficient undertaking. Sampling of domains so as to include broad geographic representation, examples of purportedly innovative designs as well as of traditional designs, and those intended to serve different population subgroups (for example, age, stage in life cycle, ethnicity), provides one basis for selecting among the many possibilities.

The ability of users to exercise control over their environment and to adapt it to meet their personal needs is also an important criterion for identifying domains to be evaluated. There are users, such as the very young, the very old, the physically or developmentally disabled, as well as those who live and work in extreme or unforgiving environments such as submarines, space craft, deserts, and the Arctic, who are more dependent on the physical environment, not only for a satisfactory life, but frequently for the very sustenance of life. These environments should be evaluated.

Three case studies are presented in this chapter that are illustrative of several of the suggested criteria for identifying and selecting environments for postconstruction evaluation. The first study is an evaluation of visitor centers in

National Parks. It is a comparative evaluation of twelve centers selected according to geographical, thematic, and design-style criteria. The second study is of a public housing project that was heralded at the time of construction as innovative and exemplary. The evaluation criteria derive from the architectural program and from the social and economic assumptions that guided the development of the design. The third study is a quasi-experimental investigation of the effects of residential building renovation on the behaviors of the residents and staff of an institution for the developmentally disabled. This study compares behaviors in pre- and post-renovation conditions.

NATIONAL PARK VISITOR CENTERS

Visitor centers have become a familiar and expected feature in many national parks, as well as in some state and regional parks. A number of functions are usually associated with these facilities: dissemination of information about park resources; orientation points for first-time visitors; interpretation of park resources and park themes (historical, natural, and recreational) through both static exhibits and dynamic audio-visual programs; provision of rest-room facilities; and, frequently, provision of space for park administrative offices.

Within the National Park Service (NPS) there have been three major periods of visitor-center design and construction. The first period was in the 1930s. It was a time of physical development in the western parks, including the building of hotels and roads. During this period automobile travel in the parks was beginning to be recognized and accommodated. The second period was associated with the "Mission 66" program and spanned the decade of 1956 to 1966. The intent of this program was to redress the lack of attention directed to national parks during and immediately after World War II, and to provide, by 1966, a range of facilities that would make the parks more accessible to the public. The design and construction of visitor centers was an important component of this activity. Several centers designed during "Mission 66" were not completed, however, until the late 1960s, due to funding and construction delays. The third period of visitor-center construction was associated with the 1976 Bicentennial celebration. The emphasis was on historical parks in the eastern United States, such as Minute Man National Historical Park in Massachusetts.

The case study presented below is a comparative evaluation of twelve NPS visitor centers selected from broadly diverse geographic regions, from different construction periods, and from the three dominant park themes—natural, historical, and recreational (Zube, Crystal, & Palmer, 1976; Zube, Palmer, & Crystal, 1977). The study was designed using a conceptual framework similar to the evaluation schema introduced in Chapter 1, consisting of institutional, environmental, and participatory dimensions. The institutional dimension was identified as the *design activity* and included a review of the design process for each center including, whenever possible, identification of decision-makers at critical steps. The environmental dimension was subdivided into *context*, and *setting*.

Context was defined as the broader environment within which the centers exist. *Setting* was defined as the specific facilities involved. For this study, *contexts* ranged from coastal sand dunes to alpine tundra. *Users* were defined to include not only visitors, but also staff and employees—thus encompassing both the daily user who works there and the occasional or one-time visitor.

The primary objective of the study was to "develop information which can contribute to more enlightened and informed design decisions in the future, and in so doing, to identify components or attributes which contribute to or detract from the quality of the centers" (Zube, Crystal, & Palmer, 1976, p. 1). Components or attributes were considered to be physical (for example, size, location, materials), perceptual (for example, aesthetics, appropriateness), and procedural (for example, design decisions).

Design programs for many of the centers were unavailable or, perhaps, for some of the older facilities, never existed. There was, however, a draft document prepared early in the "Mission 66" program that provided general guidelines for visitor center design and indicated basic NPS assumptions about use patterns (Cabot, 1958). Primary functional areas were identified as reception (entry and information), assembly (lectures and audio-visual), exhibits, and rest rooms. The optimum circulation pattern was proposed as sequential from reception through assembly to exhibits. An additional implicit assumption among NPS staff was that the primary reason many, if not most, users go to visitor centers is for the rest-room facilities. Another important element in the design of NPS facilities, including visitor centers, is the emphasis on the use of multidisciplinary teams.

Visitor Centers Studied

Visitor centers were selected for inclusion in the study so as to provide: (1) geographic distribution throughout the continental United States; (2) representation of natural, historic, and recreational park themes; (3) examples from the three major construction periods—1930s, "Mission 66," and Bicentennial; and (4) variability in the quality of the centers. The Minute Man National Historical Park Visitor Center was to have been included as representative of the Bicentennial construction period; however, construction was not completed in time and the Gettysburg National Military Park Cyclorama Center was substituted. Qualitative variability was sought by asking each of the Regional Offices of the NPS to nominate centers from their region that knowledgeable professional staff generally agreed were exceptionally good and exceptionally bad. The centers that were finally included in the study are indicated in Table 7-1.

Multiple Methods

Table 7-2 presents a list of the major issues that were investigated and the study methods that were employed. The documents that were analyzed included, when available, the prospectus for the visitor center interpretive program, the

Table 7-1. Visitor Centers Selected for Study

	Date of Construction	Theme			Location— NPS Region (State)	Architect
		Natural	Historical	Recreational		
Bandelier NM	1935	X			Southwest (New Mexico)	Unknown
Cape Cod NS-Province Lands	1967			X	North Atlantic (Mass.)	B. Biderman (NPS)
Fort Raleigh NHS	1966		X		Southeast (N.C.)	L. Biond (NPS)
Gettysburg NMP-Cyclorama	1962		X		Mid-Atlantic (Penn.)	Neutra and Alexander Los Angeles, California
Great Falls Park	1966	X			Nat'l. Capitol Parks (Va)	Kent Cooper Associates Washington, D.C.
Olympic NP-Hoh	1965	X			Pacific Northwest (Wa.)	C. Doty (NPS)
Petersburg NB	1967		X		Mid-Atlantic (Va)	B. Biderman (NPS)
Rocky Mountain NP-Alpine	1965	X			Rocky Mountain (Colo.)	W. Muchow, Denver, Colo.
Rocky Mountain NP-Headquarters	1968	X			Rocky Mountain (Colo.)	Taliesen Associates Architects, Ltd., Ariz.
Scotts Bluff NM	1935		X		Midwest (Neb.)	H. Baker (NPS)
Wright Brothers NM	1960		X		Southeast (N.C.)	Mitchell and Guirgola Philadelphia, Pa.
Yosemite NP-Valley	1965	X			Western (California)	Spencer Associates Palo Alto, Calif.

(NPS) indicates that the architect worked for the National Park Service.
From *Visitor Center Design Evaluation*, by E. H. Zube, J. H. Crystal, and J. F. Palmer. Copyright 1976 by the University of Massachusetts.
Reprinted by permission of The Environmental Institute, University of Massachusetts at Amherst.

Table 7-2. Evaluation Issues and Methods

Evaluation Issues	Methods				
	Document Analysis	*Interview*	*Check List*	*Systematic Observation*	*Questionnaire*
Spatial allocation	x				
Circulation-flow patterns				x	x
Intensity of use-crowding				x	x
Building alterations	x	x			
Maintenance issues		x	x	x	
Barrier-free access			x		
Safety and security		x	x		
Building aesthetics				x	
Exhibit quality	x			x	
A-V program quality	x			x	

park master plan, working drawings for the site and building, and the task directive or building design program. In addition to identifying the intended functional allocation of space (exhibit rooms, offices, rest rooms, auditorium, reception area) and the intent of the interpretive program (exhibits and audio-visual), the document review also pointed out where building alterations had subsequently been made to accommodate changing needs and patterns of use.

Interviews were conducted with the park superintendents, chiefs of interpretation, and chiefs of maintenance, and were intended to elicit and document knowledge about the use and functioning of visitor centers and the "conventional wisdoms" that can only be acquired through the kinds of experiences shared by these people. Check lists were used to provide a structured way of observing and assessing important physical attributes of the environment, such as potentially hazardous design features and barriers to free access for the handicapped.

Questionnaires were administered to 3065 visitors at the twelve centers and to 150 NPS employees who work in the centers. The questionnaires were intended to provide information on users' perceptions of building interiors and exteriors as well as of exhibits and audio-visual programs, and on activities or behaviors within the building and the park. Systematic observation of users—of who was engaged in what kinds of activities at what places and at what times —provided objective data for comparison with subjective questionnaire responses on user activity. As indicated in Table 7-2, data on a number of issues were obtained by using more than one method.

Users

Who were the visitors that participated in the study, and how were they selected? The geographic distribution of the centers and the size of the research budget precluded the use of a random-sample design. Instead, peak visitation days were identified and selected for each center. Peak days were selected because they represent the conditions under which a majority of visitors experience the centers. Questionnaires were distributed hourly, with the number per hour being generally proportional to the frequency distribution of visitors over time per day. The visitors who completed the questionnaire were generally young (mean age of 31.9), well educated (63.4% had some college education), frequent visitors to NPS areas (83% had been to at least two other areas in the previous three years), and had traveled a considerable distance (63% had traveled more than 300 miles).

Table 7-3. Main Reason for Going to Visitor Center

Visitor Center	*(Percent of Total Respondents)*							
	Obtain Information	*Look Around*	*View Exhibits*	*Use Rest Rooms*	*See Audio/ Visual Program*	*With Someone*	*Sit and Rest*	*Other*
Bandelier NM	34.3	32.1	18.7	.7	3.7	3.7	—	6.0
Cape Cod NS-Province Lands	30.5	47.0	4.6	6.3	3.0	2.3	3.6	2.3
Fort Raleigh NHS	21.6	43.2	16.0	7.2	4.0	3.2	.8	4.0
Gettysburg NMP-Cyclorama	10.9	31.8	32.8	1.5	16.9	1.5	—	4.5
Great Falls Park	19.4	46.7	8.5	4.8	5.5	2.4	3.6	9.1
Olympic NP-Hoh	40.5	32.4	14.3	5.7	1.0*	2.4	—	3.8
Petersburg NB	18.4	31.2	36.0	1.6	11.2	—	—	1.6
Rocky Mountain NP-Alpine	9.5	52.7	17.1	11.3	.7*	.7	1.8	6.2
Rocky Mountain NP-Headquarters	52.2	14.3	4.4	6.4	12.3	1.5	.5	8.4
Scotts Bluff NM	11.0	40.2	33.9	1.6	2.4*	.8	4.7	6.5
Wright Brothers NM	8.5	34.2	47.3	.9	2.5	4.1	—	2.5
Yosemite NP-Valley	34.8	28.1	24.8	1.7	1.0	1.7	.3	7.6
Mean ($\bar{X}$)	24.3	36.4	21.7	4.3	4.8	2.1	1.2	5.1

*There are no full audio/visual programs at these parks. However, Alpine does have an audio tape and Scotts Bluff a living history program.

From *Visitor Center Design Evaluation*, by E. H. Zube, J. H. Crystal, and J. F. Palmer. Copyright 1976 by the University of Massachusetts. Reprinted by permission of The Environmental Institute, University of Massachusetts at Amherst.

Table 7-4. First Destination After Entry

Visitor Center	Percentages								
	Reception					Rest Rooms		Other	
	Information	*Sales*	*Rest Area*	*Exhibits*	*Auditorium*	*Rest Rooms*	*Fountain*	*Observation Area*	*Other*
Bandelier NM	38	0	4	39	5	6	1	3	4
Cape Cod NS-Province Lands	27	0	2	38	4	18	0	8	4
Fort Raleigh NHS	35	0	1	38	12	10	0	0	5
Gettysburg NMP-Cyclorama	46	0	0	30	14	8	1	0	1
Great Falls Park	27	0	8	36	8	11	1	0	10
Olympic NP-Hoh	20	0	3	53	0	22	0	0	2
Petersburg NB	25	0	2	50	20	3	0	0	1
Rocky Mountain NP-Alpine	18	1	2	28	3	39	1	7	1
Rocky Mountain NP-Headquarters	38	0	2	29	10	18	0	1	3
Scotts Bluff NM	28	1	6	47	0	10	1	4	3
Wright Brothers NM	17	1	1	53	10	16	1	0	1
Yosemite NP-Valley	33	1	1	55	1	6	0	2	2

From *Visitor Center Design Evaluation*, by E. H. Zube, J. H. Crystal, and J. F. Palmer. Copyright 1976 by the University of Massachusetts. Reprinted by permission of the Environmental Institute, University of Massachusetts at Amherst.

Selected Findings

While the study produced considerable data derived from sources other than users, the selected findings discussed here will be limited primarily to those gleaned from interviews, questionnaires, and observation.

Tables 7-3 and 7-4, respectively, indicate the main reason given by visitors for going to a center and the first place they went after entering. The implicit assumption that people go to centers primarily to use the toilets was not substantiated by these self reports. Only at Rocky Mountain Alpine Center did more than 10% indicate use of rest rooms as a main reason. It should be noted, however, that the drive to the center is of considerable length and is accompanied by significant changes in elevation and temperature, all of which produces a not unpredictable response in many people. The reported first destinations of visitors also suggest that the proposed optimum sequential circulation pattern was frequently not followed, with major percentages of visitors going to exhibits before stopping in either the reception area or the auditorium. Interviews with staff also indicated that frequently, during peak periods, they influenced circulation patterns by directing visitors to less-crowded areas or by rescheduling audio-visual programs.

Visitors' perceptions of the quality of the facilities were, in general, positive, but they did discriminate among the components. Building interiors and exteriors, exhibits, and audio-visual programs appear to have been judged independently. If the exhibit material did not match the quality of the building and/or the audio-visual program, visitors' responses indicated a sensitivity to this qualitative disparity. Staff consistently perceived the facilities as of lower quality than did visitors. Only one center was perceived by either staff or visitors as slightly below average, however—Yosemite Valley—and that was only by the staff. Perhaps the greater familiarity of staff with the facilities accounts for their somewhat less enthusiastic response to the centers.

Historic theme centers were generally perceived by visitors as more suitable and satisfying than natural or recreational theme centers. In some respects this is not surprising, as the subject matter is frequently more easily accommodated in exhibit format than are the grandeur and natural processes of Yosemite Valley or the Rocky Mountains. Visitors may also associate history more with exhibits and museums, and nature more with participation or in situ viewing.

A comparison of questionnaire responses and observation data suggested that visitors began to sense a feeling of being crowded when densities approached one person per sixteen to twenty square feet. Whether or not this sense of crowdedness affected visitor satisfaction was not clear.

Finally, all of the data indicated that visitor centers that were designed using a team approach were generally perceived to be better than those where a team approach was not used. The interaction of architect, exhibit designer, interior designer, and landscape architect resulted in facilities where all components were perceived to be of high quality.

EASTER HILL VILLAGE

Easter Hill Village is a public-housing project in Richmond, California that was built in 1954. Shortly after being built it was recognized in professional journals as an important and innovative contribution to public-housing design. In 1957, it was cited by the American Institute of Architects as one of the Ten Buildings in America's Future, and in 1964 it received an award for design and excellence from the Housing and Home Finance Agency of the Public Housing Administration (Cooper, 1975, p. 8). These are impressive citations for a public-housing project. Most often, such projects are better known for their limited budgets and austere designs. It is important to note, however, that the accolades directed to Easter Hill Village were given by architects and housing administrators. Cooper (1975) undertook the task of obtaining a user evaluation of the housing in 1964, ten years after the project was completed. Were the users as satisfied with the housing as were the architectural critics?

The project architects—Donald L. Hardison and Vernon DeMars—had responsibility for assisting in the selection of the site for the housing as well as for the design of the project. The site that was finally selected was a small hill of 21.5 acres in an otherwise flat area of Richmond. The surrounding neighborhood was drab, with poorly maintained single-family homes, litter-strewn vacant lots, warehouses, scattered businesses and, on two sides, heavily travelled streets, including considerable truck traffic.

Design Objectives

The architects had definite ideas about the kind of housing that was suitable for families with children. These ideas were based on the designers' assumptions about the values and life-styles of public-housing residents, and constituted the basis for a set of design objectives:

1. to avoid the institutional image of existing public-housing projects
2. to provide each family with a house of its own
3. to give each family control over a piece of private outdoor space
4. to provide means for the expression of individuality in and around the home
5. to foster neighborliness and casual encounters among residents
6. to fulfill children's needs for individual/adventurous play and for group/field sports
7. to create self-identified subgroups in the community by the arrangement of clusters of dwellings.

The client for the project, the Richmond Housing Authority, also had a set of objectives. In addition to the obvious one of providing more public housing, they were:

1. to keep building costs to a minimum
2. to keep landscaping costs to a minimum
3. to keep maintenance costs to a minimum

The Project Environment

The designers' objectives addressed the social context of a public-housing environment, while the client's objectives addressed the costs of constructing and maintaining the project. The environment that resulted from these combined objectives consisted of 300 row-house units: 36 one-bedroom; 150 two-bedroom; 90 three-bedroom; and 24 four-bedroom. Each unit had a front yard and a back yard. Buildings, parking lots, and streets covered 41% of the 21.5 acres. Yard space and public open space accounted for 22% and 37% of the area, respectively. The street pattern was curvilinear and included cul-de-sacs. Window and door arrangements, porch designs, and house colors were varied to provide greater individuality in house facades. Large boulders encountered in construction were retained as visual landscape elements and play features for children. Streets and building locations were oriented inward, turning their backs on the surrounding neighborhood. The resulting environment stood out in sharp contrast to its drab surroundings.

From Objectives to Evaluation

Each of the design objectives represents a set of assumptions that the architects held about the project. In initiating the evaluation study, Cooper interviewed the architects to identify these assumptions about user needs and find out how the assumptions were presumed to be fulfilled through physical design. A set of questions was then designed to probe users' perceptions of the physical environment and to assess possible discrepancies between designers' assumptions about what the residents wanted and what the residents say they want. Table 7-5 illustrates the relationships among assumptions, physical solutions, and questions asked of residents, in relation to the objective of providing each family with a house of its own.

The designers also had to devise solutions that were responsive to their client's cost-related objectives, and to consider the social consequences of their solutions. Table 7-6 illustrates the relationships among physical solutions, hypothesized social consequences, and questions asked of residents, in relation to the objective of minimizing maintenance costs.

The Interviews and the Respondents

The interview schedule constructed by Cooper addressed four kinds of issues or topics: (1) coincidence of the residents' needs and wants with the social objectives of the designers; (2) the Easter Hill environment; (3) housing and the general residential environment; and (4) general demographic background. The structured schedule consisted of both fixed-response and open-ended questions. In addition, the interviewers compiled notes based on their insights and observations.

A random sample of households was selected, and 52 interviews were conducted. Ninety percent of the respondents were female. Forty-two percent were minorities, and fifty-eight percent were Caucasian. Sixty-nine percent were under forty years of age, and twenty-seven percent were divorced or separated, four percent were widowed, and six percent were single. There was an average of two children per household. Ten of the females in the sampled households had outside employment, and twenty-nine of the males held skilled, unskilled, or serviceman positions. Three males were in clerical or professional positions, six were unemployed, and seventeen households were without an adult male.

Table 7-5 Design Objective: To Provide Each Family with a Home of Its Own

Assumptions Regarding the Fulfillment of User Needs Through Physical Design	Physical Solution	Questions Asked of Residents
A "home" implies a house, not an apartment.	Dwelling units for families are provided in semidetached and row houses; the only apartments are for single, elderly persons (i.e., nonnuclear families).	If you could live in any of these neighborhoods for the same rent you are paying here, which would you choose? [four photographs shown]
A row house is perceived as a house and not as an apartment.	Each unit (except walk-ups) has a private front path and porch, and a private back path and porch.	Do you think you'd like the house if there were some space between it and the houses on either side? Why?
Although basically similar, row houses with private front and back entrances and varied exterior detailing will be perceived as being different and individual by their inhabitants.	Each house is slightly different in exterior detailing and/or setback from its neighbor.	Some people prefer it when all the houses in a neighborhood look the same, and others like it better when there are differences between the houses. What do you feel about this?
A house that is perceived as being physically individual and different from its neighbors will, even though rented and attached, give the inhabitants a sense of having "a home of their own."		Do you think the houses here have differences between them or do they look all the same? In what ways do they look different from each other?
A house that is perceived as being individual and different is therefore preferable to one that looks like its neighbors.		Do you like having a covered front porch? Why? What do you use it for?
		Which is more important to you—the appearance of the *inside* of the house, or the outside? Why?
		What sort of house/apartment did you live in before moving here? How do you feel about it, compared with this house?

Table 7-6. Economic Objective: To Keep Maintenance Costs to a Minimum

Physical Solution	Hypothesized Social Consequences	Questions Asked of Residents
Front and side yards are fairly limited in extent so that they can be easily maintained by the tenants themselves.	Residents' dwellings will be perceived more as homes since they have a piece of open space attached to take care of.	Do you like looking after the front yard yourself, or would you rather the Housing Authority took care of it for you?
A considerable proportion of the total open space is in private fenced yards, which represent no maintenance cost to the Housing Authority.	Residents will appreciate the "extra" of a private back yard.	How do you like having a fenced back yard? What do you use it for?
Almost all the public open space is grassed (no ground cover, bushes, etc.), hence relatively cheap to maintain.	Residents will appreciate the greenness and openness of the neighborhood.	Is it important for you to see trees and grass in the neighborhood where you live? Do you think this is an attractive neighborhood to look at? Do you feel that the Housing Authority takes good care of Easter Hill—the streets, the trees, etc.?

Reprinted with permission of Macmillan Publishing Co., Inc. from *Easter Hill Village*, by C. C. Cooper. Copyright © 1975 by The Free Press, a Division of Macmillan Publishing Co., Inc.

Summary of the Findings

Interviews and interviewers' notes indicated that the physical solutions devised to meet both the architects' social objectives and the Housing Authority's cost objectives were not always successful. With the possible exception of the objective to create self-identified subgroups in the community by the arrangement of clusters of dwellings, the architects' social objectives were appropriate and responsive to felt needs of the residents. Cooper speculates that self-identified subgroups or social groupings, when they did occur, were more a function of common socioeconomic backgrounds or shared views on childrearing, or shared perceptions of the desirability of their part of the project over other areas.

The physical solutions designed to meet the objectives of (1) providing control over a piece of private outdoor space (for example, a fenced back yard, unfenced front yard, and/or a front porch); (2) providing a means for expressing individuality in and around the home (for example, arrangement of furniture and possessions, care of front yard); and (3) fostering neighborliness and casual encounters among residents (arrangements of houses around courts, network of pedestrian walkways, unfenced front yards) were in general successful. With a few exceptions, these assumptions of the architects about what residents would want were supported by what they actually wanted.

The objective of providing each family with a house of its own was an appropriate one—it was what residents wanted. However, the efforts to create a sense of individual houses (primarily through variations in the facades) were not successful. The designers' objective of avoiding an institutional image was not realized either, at least as the project was perceived by the respondents. Respondents liked Easter Hill better than other projects, but row housing was perceived as institutional and mass-produced. It is important to note that the respondents were not concerned about any social stigma attached to living in the project. Perhaps this objective was not as important, therefore, as others.

The least successful effort to match physical solutions to assumptions and social objectives was in the provision of play spaces and opportunities for children. The saving of boulders as play features was successful, but the location of the play field and the use of many small play areas scattered among the houses were not. The play field did not serve all areas of the project equally, and the small play areas adjacent to the houses led to complaints about noisy play right under the windows—a problem that was probably compounded by an underestimation of the number of children in the project.

The client's cost objectives and the resultant physical solutions also met with variable success. Keeping building costs at a minimum, particularly in public housing projects, leads to inevitable compromises. For example, at Easter Hill it meant compromising on interior space and not providing storage, lack of individuality among units, no community buildings, and lack of soundproofing in party walls between adjacent units. Obviously, as noted previously, some of these limitations also affected the architects' ability to more adequately meet social objectives. Physical solutions designed to keep landscaping costs to a minimum had both positive and negative effects. The retention of the boulders was an excellent idea. However, the limited budget precluded the planting of adequate numbers of trees and shrubs for privacy. Such plantings could also have enhanced the aesthetic qualities of the project, as well as making a probable contribution to several other social objectives, such as individuality and noninstitutional image. The designers' decision to reduce maintenance costs by including a considerable amount of the available open space in private yards was successful from several points of view. First, it did reduce project maintenance costs (but added to residents' costs) and, second, it contributed considerably to the residents' satisfaction with the project as a place to live.

Some Conclusions

Overall, when respondents were asked what they liked most about Easter Hill, they mentioned their neighbors more frequently than physical features. When asked what they disliked, however, physical features ranked first.

Cooper suggests that public decision-makers and other professionals responsible for the design and construction of public housing are negligent in the lack of attention directed to the design and maintenance of the spaces between buildings, spaces that contribute in important ways to the quality of multifamily neighborhoods. Her overall recommendation, recognizing that low-income people occupy underprivileged social positions, is that low-cost housing should resemble as nearly as possible, average, middle-class family housing.

ENVIRONMENT FOR THE DEVELOPMENTALLY DISABLED

During the early 1970s, attitudes toward the care and treatment of the developmentally disabled began to change. The predominant practice of institutional confinement for such persons was questioned, and alternatives to this practice were sought. The concept of normalization began to gain acceptance as an alternative practice (Wolfensberger, 1973).

The normalization concept is not well defined. Implicit in this notion, however, is the assumption that normal environments foster and facilitate adaptive behaviors. Normal environments are envisioned as less institutional and more homelike. These environments are believed to facilitate behavior patterns among the developmentally disabled that are perceived as more culturally normative.

The case study discussed below (Knight, Weitzer, & Zimring, 1978) investigated the assumption that normalized physical environments facilitate more socially desirable behavior. The primary focus of the study was the interaction of residents, staff, and environment in an institution for the developmentally dis-

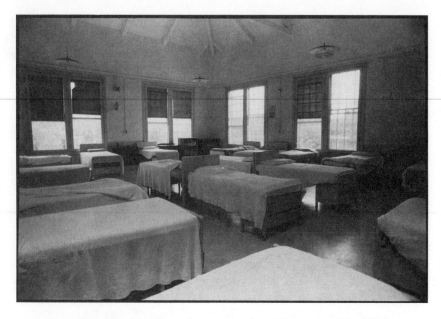

Figure 7-1. Sleeping space prior to renovation. (Photos copyright 1978 by Alyce Kaprow. Reprinted by permission of Alyce Kaprow and The Environmental Institute, University of Massachusetts at Amherst, from the book *Opportunity for Control and the Built Environment: The ELEMR Project,* by R. Christopher Knight, William H. Weitzer, and Craig M. Zimring.)

abled. The study adopted a time-series quasi-experimental design that provided for assessing changes over time within and among the residents, staff, and environment.

Financial support was provided by the U.S. Department of Health, Education and Welfare, Developmental Disabilities Office.

The Study Environment

Belchertown State School (BSS), located in rural western Massachusetts, was constructed in the 1920s and 1930s. It consists of moderate-sized buildings that accommodated 40 to 55 residents each at the time the study was started. Each building contained six spaces measuring 30′ × 40′. Three of the rooms provided sleeping space for 15 to 20 residents each (see Figure 7-1). The remaining spaces served as day rooms, dining halls, or multi-purpose rooms. The rooms were utilitarian in nature and sparsely furnished. Building materials and surfaces were durable and easily maintained. Furniture was not only sparse but frequently in disrepair. In addition, a newer building, constructed in 1968, was studied. This building had a similar open, institutional design prior to renovation.

The concern of residents' parents and the general public with these conditions resulted in a class-action suit on behalf of the residents. The court found that

Figure 7-2. Modular design with semiprivate sleeping areas.

the constitutional right of the residents to treatment had been violated. The court awarded 2.6 million dollars for physical renovations to be accomplished within an established time frame. The renovations included only building interiors. Since 1970, the population at BSS has dropped from about 1500 residents to 700 residents, with the lowest-functioning residents remaining in the institution.

Three renovation alternatives were developed for the several existing building styles. The older institutional buildings were renovated following either a modular design or a suite design, while the building constructed in 1968 was renovated following a corridor or college-dormitory design.

The modular design consisted of four and one-half foot high partitions that divided the large rooms into twelve semi-private areas and a small lounge space (see Figure 7-2). Each semi-private area included a bed, dresser/closet, desk, and mirror with corkboard. Lighting was controlled by a central switch for each large room.

The suite design consisted of eight-foot-high partitions that divided the large rooms into four four-room suites. Within each suite, three rooms were used as sleeping accommodations for two to four residents (see Figure 7-3). The fourth room was a lounge. Bedrooms were furnished with area rugs, beds, dressers, chairs, and draperies. Lights in bedrooms were individually controlled.

The dormitory design consisted of bedrooms along both sides of the corridor. Bedrooms were either singles or doubles, and were furnished with beds, dressers, closets, chairs, and mirrors (see Figure 7-4). The doors could be locked and lights were individually controlled by room occupants. In addition, the

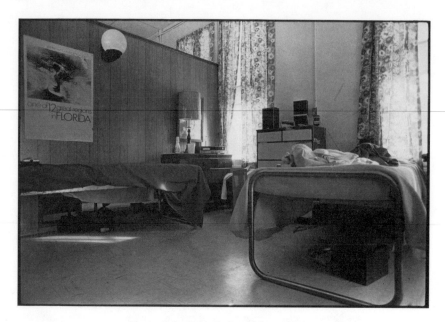

Figure 7-3. Suite design with partition.

building had several furnished lounge areas. Carpeting was used in a number of areas throughout the building.

Each of these alternatives provided varying degrees of privacy and varying opportunities for residents to exert control over their environments. The potential for privacy ranged from the maximum single bedroom with locked door to the minimum in the modular unit with only partial screening. Opportunities for control varied also from the minimum in the modular unit, to the maximum in the dormitory unit with individual light switches and door locks. It is important to note that opportunity to control one's physical environment usually means the opportunity to control one's social environment as well.

Study Participants

The residents who participated in this study had been diagnosed as severely and profoundly retarded. They were physically healthy, adult men and women who had spent most of their lives in institutions. Some required assistance in day-to-day functions such as dressing and toileting, while others were more independent.

The staff who participated were the direct-care staff, who had the greatest contact with the residents on a daily basis. They tended to be poorly paid and poorly educated. Their custodial-maintenance attitude toward their jobs was reinforced by training and by an institutional structure that emphasized physical care of residents.

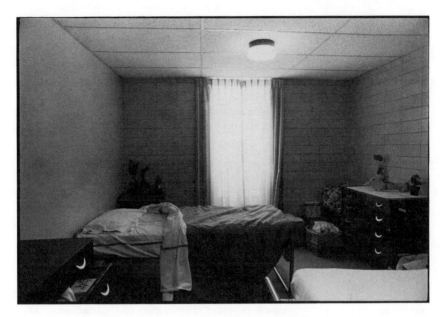

Figure 7-4. Dormitory design, double bedroom.

Study Design

Several important attributes characterized this study. First, it was longitudinal, spanning a period of four years; second, it employed multiple and converging methods, with a heavy emphasis on observation; and, third, emphasis was placed on the construct or idea of *control* as an important variable mediating the effect of environment on behavior.

The three central questions addressed in the study were:

1. Did the staff and residents use, recognize, and respect personal/private spaces?
2. Did staff-resident interactions improve?
3. What was the effect of renovations on resident social and solitary behaviors? (Knight, Weitzer, & Zimring, 1978, p. 21)

Emphasis was placed on the direct observation of behavior as a primary research technique. Over the four years of the study, 300,000 coded observations were obtained. Six observation periods of about six weeks each were conducted. Prerenovation baseline data for the residents and several buildings were collected in from one to three observation periods scheduled four to eight months apart. At the time of the postrenovation observation periods, residents and staff had been in the new environments for anywhere from six to twelve months.

Behavioral observations of residents were classified in the following categories:

1. Residents' use of their own personal/private spaces
2. Residents' intrusions into others' personal/private spaces
3. Resident-staff interactions
4. Resident-resident interactions
5. Resident-resident positive social interactions (subcategory of 4)
6. Resident verbal interactions
7. Resident-resident verbal interactions (subcategory of 6)
8. Alert
9. Withdrawn

Behavioral observations of staff were classified in the following categories:

1. Staff intrusions into residents' personal/private spaces
2. Staff unjustified intrusions into residents' personal/private spaces
3. Staff initiated interactions with residents
4. Resident initiated interactions with staff
5. Interaction context: personal care, ward activity, formal training, or social

Direct observation of behavior was supplemented with other methods: participant and nonparticipant observation; interviewing of staff and administration, including use of the "critical incidents" technique (perceived incidents of positive and negative behavior); speech-discrimination experiments and acoustic measurement (the effects of noise on the ability to discriminate between similar sounding words such as hand, man, and sand); and content analysis of institutional records. Figure 7-5 indicates the temporal relationships among these multiple methods.

Over the four-year time frame, nine different buildings were observed from one to five times each; 141 individual residents and 50 direct-care staff were observed. The final analysis of the data was conducted using a sample of four buildings, 92 residents, and 33 direct-care staff. The sample allowed for clearer comparisons among settings and, therefore, more informed analyses of the findings.

Overall, the study can best be described as following an ethological perspective. It placed heavy emphasis on observation, and it employed an inductive strategy. Rather than defining and testing hypotheses, hypotheses were based on actual observations in the institution.

Results and Conclusions

A study of this magnitude provides an immense volume of valuable data that challenges the researchers' analytical capabilities. The opportunities to analyze relationships among sets of relevant variables appear limitless. The following paragraphs represent a very modest sampling of the impressive output of this study. Attention is directed specifically to findings related to the three central questions of the study and to one of the previously stated important

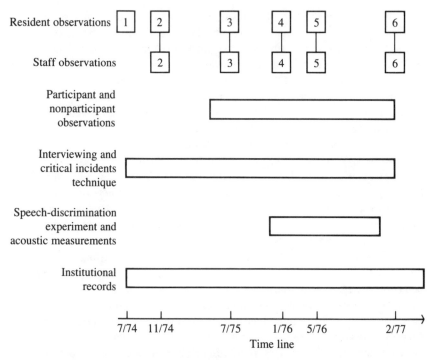

Figure 7-5. Time-line of multiple methods used. (Adapted from *Opportunity for Control and the Built Environment: The ELEMR Project,* by R. Christopher Knight, William H. Weitzer, and Craig M. Zimring. Copyright 1978 by the University of Massachusetts. Reprinted by permission of The Environmental Institute, University of Massachusetts at Amherst.)

attributes of the study, the construct of control as a variable that mediates the effect of environment on behavior.

Did the staff and residents use, recognize, and respect personal/private spaces? The answer to this question, in relation to the modular design was a definitive *no,* while there were significant changes in this respect in relation to the suite and corridor, or dormitory, designs. However, staff intrusions into residents' personal/private space in the suite design increased over time, from a low immediately after renovation to nearly the levels of before renovation. A similar pattern prevailed with residents' intrusions into other residents' space.

Did staff-resident interactions improve? Interactions did change, but the answer to the question of improvement is ambiguous. There was a modest increase in resident-staff interaction in the modular design, but it was one-way interaction initiated by the staff. The overall increase in interactions was also found to be due to staff initiations with higher-functioning residents. In both the suite and the corridor designs, however, staff-resident interactions decreased to a very low level, below that in the unrenovated facilities. This was attributed to the staff's ability to withdraw from residents in the renovated environment.

What was the effect of renovations on resident social and solitary behaviors? The modular design had no effect on resident-resident behaviors and no lasting effect on solitary behaviors. Resident-resident interactions increased in both the suite and corridor designs; however, the overall level was higher in the suite than in the corridor. There was an increase in verbal interactions in both designs, in part, perhaps, because of the improved acoustical environment, with a greater increase in the corridor design. Increases in alertness and decreases in withdrawn behaviors were noted in both designs with larger positive changes noted in the corridor design than in the suite design.

Knight, Weitzer, and Zimring conclude: "Even very poorly functioning developmentally disabled residents exhibited improved social and solitary behavior in more home-like environments. However, the effects of the built environment were primarily mediated by the staff responses to the environment and by the extent to which the residents were allowed to realize control over their environmental experiences" (p. 130).

"The corridor design building was clearly more effective than the suite, the modular, or the institutional designs in facilitating a variety of positive social behaviors and general alertness" (p. 130).

"The corridor design was clearly the 'best' renovation for these clients. However, it is critically important not to misconstrue the reasons for its relative success. The corridor design was not an ideal built environment and in fact was quite institutional. Nonetheless, it did offer an appropriate level of control for the users" (p. 144).

In summary, there was improvement in social and solitary behavior of the residents—for example, as indicated by the frequency of verbal interaction with other residents, declines in withdrawn behaviors, and increases in residents' alertness. In addition, even though the corridor design was less attractive than other alternatives (in relation to furnishings, carpeting, and materials) it did provide residents with greater opportunity for control over their environment and was more supportive of improved social and solitary behaviors. Individual rooms with doors (rather than partially walled suites) provided greater opportunity to control visual and auditory privacy, light, noise, and social interactions.

LEARNING FROM THE CASE STUDIES

Among the three kinds of evaluations we have discussed, postconstruction evaluation and evaluative inventories of existing environments are probably most similar. As noted in Chapter 6, evaluations of alternative futures can present special problems, such as representing or simulating alternative futures and identifying relevant users or surrogate users of environments yet to be built. These characteristics, and others, tend to distinguish this evaluative activity from the other two. There are, nevertheless, several characteristics, primarily institutional, that distinguish many postconstruction evaluations from inventory evaluations. In the following discussions, these characteristics will be identified, in addition to the analysis of salient features of the three case studies.

The Institutional Dimension

Each of the studies was undertaken with the intention of providing feedback to the design process. A significant difference among them, however, is that two were done for specific clients while one, the Easter Hill study, was done as a masters degree project and did not have a specific client. Whether or not the existence of a specific client makes a difference in the findings of a study being used in future designs is not an easy question to answer. One hopes that it would—that is, that an office or agency interested enough to fund a study would also be interested in using the results to improve its design process. There are, however, relatively few examples on which to base any kind of conclusion. To date, a considerable number of the postconstruction evaluations have been undertaken by faculty and students in environmental design fields and social/behavioral sciences (see Friedmann, Zimring, & Zube, 1978). It is a rare design contract that includes, as part of the process, a postconstruction evaluation. Funding for such studies has been difficult to obtain.

The BSS study of an environment for the developmentally disabled certainly provides important information for the designer of residential facilities for the mentally retarded; its primary purpose, however, was more basic. It was to investigate whether more normal environments are associated with more normal behaviors.

The findings from the three studies, and the way in which they were presented, should have utility for decision-makers and designers. Cooper developed a comprehensive list of design guidelines for housing, drawing on her Easter Hill findings and an extensive survey of the literature. In other words, her guidelines represented a synthesis of housing-evaluation research, using the Easter Hill study as a primary source. Guidelines ranged from site considerations, general building design, and specific room design, to privacy, maintenance, and security. Recommendations resulting from the visitor center study were organized according to the conceptual framework that was used in the conduct of the study. In scope, they encompassed the same range of concerns for visitor centers as did the housing guidelines. In addition, recommendations were included relating to the thematic and geographical context of the visitor centers and to the design process (that is, the importance of design teams). The BSS study included a set of recommendations oriented to the concept of opportunity for control. The recommendations addressed such issues as the size of residential groups, distinctions between public and private spaces, resident participation in selecting furnishings, professional designers' roles, resident-staff ratios, staff training, staff responsibilities, and staff facilities. Recommendations were directed specifically to administrators, policy-makers, and designers.

The evaluation strategies followed in the three studies were markedly different. The Easter Hill study relied primarily on interviews as an information source. The visitor center study employed multiple methods, including interviews, check lists, systematic observation, and questionnaires. The questionnaires included fixed-response questions and rating scales as well as photographic representations of other visitor centers for purposes of aesthetic comparisons. The advantage of multiple study methods is that one can compare what people say they do with what they actually do, and one can try to identify behavioral patterns that are valid indicators of user satisfaction, such as the length of time spent in a visitor center. The BSS study also employed multiple methods, but given the limited verbal skills of one important sector of the study population, primary emphasis was placed on observation.

Postconstruction evaluations are usually defined in terms of specific buildings or projects. Evaluative inventories, on the other hand, are usually undertaken as a part of planning or monitoring activities that encompass larger geographic areas and multiple domains. The explicit, institutional sponsorship of evaluative inventories as a part of the design process provides a more direct link to decision-makers and should provide a higher probability of study findings being used in decision-making—notwithstanding the policy/practice gap discussed in Chapter 3. The explicit inclusion of such studies in the design process also means an identifiable source of funds to support the studies—an element critically missing in postconstruction studies, as noted previously.

The Environmental Dimension

While the domains of the three studies were defined, respectively, as visitor centers, public housing, and an institution, the first two studies were designed to encompass a larger geographic context. The visitor center study was placed within the context of the total park, the park theme (historical, recreational, or natural), and the surrounding environment. The Easter Hill study was placed within the context of the surrounding environment, thus encompassing varying project contexts from the individual dwelling unit and micro neighborhood to the larger community. Implicit in this notion of domain and surrounding context is the assumption that domain boundaries are permeable and that users' perceptions of and experiences in a specific housing project or visitor center are influenced by perceptions of and experiences in the surrounding environment. In contrast, the residents of BSS are limited in their geographic range of experiences to their immediate environs.

The three studies differ in some respects in the derivation of standards, criteria, and measurement systems. The Easter Hill study demonstrates admirably the value of a documented architectural program, in this case one that was specified in terms of social values and desired life-styles. These program assumptions served as the basis for the evaluation; they provided the standards and criteria to which user perceptions were related. Thus, both the design program and the physical environment are the subject of the evaluation. Without the link between evaluation and design program, case studies of single projects such as Easter Hill lose much of their potential value as feedback instruments to the design process. Understanding of why something happened and who made the decision is important if the process is to be improved.

Design programs were not available for most of the visitor centers, although there were some general concepts and assumptions about circulation and patterns of use to serve as minimal evaluation standards. In the absence of design programs and more comprehensive standards and criteria, the comparison among centers provided an internally consistent basis for evaluation. The qualities of the visitor centers were not determined on the basis of how close users' perceptions agreed with designers' programs. Rather, the measurement of quality employed a relative scale that was defined by the qualitative range of the various center components across the twelve centers. The qualities of individual centers or groups of centers are relative to the perceived qualities of all the centers.

The BSS study provided an important comparative study of four environments for the mentally retarded. The primary evaluation criterion for the study was the change to more socially desirable social and solitary behaviors, from the nonrenovated to the post-renovation condition in each of the designs. The measurement of quality was related to the concept of more normal environments and more normal behavior.

Physical attributes were defined similarly in all studies as subunits or components of the domain—room, porch, yard, and neighborhood in the Easter Hill study; reception, assembly, exhibit, and rest-room areas in the visitor center study; and wall heights, locus of light control, doors and room materials and furnishings in the BSS study. Interviews in the Easter Hill and visitor center studies, however, indicated that not only must physical characteristics and components be considered, but also that it is equally important (or perhaps more important, in some cases) to consider the set of social variables or characteristics that are a part of the same environmental domain. At Easter Hill these variables and characteristics would include such factors as friendliness of neighbors, management policies, maintenance, and security, and, in visitor centers, administrative decisions to alter the flow of visitors or to shorten audio-visual programs, and the interpersonal relations between staff and visitors. The BSS study consciously addressed the issue of the roles others play as mediating variables in achieving environmental goals and objectives. These social variables can and do influence our perceptions of the quality of our environments.

The Participatory Dimension

The identification of the users at Easter Hill was accomplished in a straightforward manner. The users were the residents. At the visitor centers, users were more broadly defined to include center staff, maintenance people, and park administrators, as well as visitors to the parks. This breadth of user definition provided valuable information that would not otherwise have been available. The users of BSS were defined as the residents and the direct-care staff.

The users of Easter Hill and BSS are year-round users, while the majority of those at visitor centers are short-term users (fifteen minutes to one hour). It is reasonable to assume that the behaviors and perceptions of year-round users represent their cumulative thoughts, feelings, and experiences with the environment. It may not be reasonable to assume, however, that the perceptions of peak visitation-time users of visitor centers are the same as those of off-season users, particularly if off-season users tend to be representative of other population subgroups, such as retired or older people who take off-season vacations to avoid crowds. Had resources permitted, the visitor center study would have benefited from sampling users over all seasons.

The housing study employed a random-sample design for the identification of participants. The BSS study included the total population of selected buildings. Generalization of the findings from the visitor center study is more limited because of the opportunity sampling procedures employed. This limitation is somewhat alleviated by the large number of participants in the total study.

Finally, the first two studies are cross-sectional studies, as are those in Chapters 5 and 6—that is, they represent users' perceptions of the quality of various environments or proposals at one point in time. In contrast, the BSS study sampled behaviors and perceptions over a four-year period. The epilogue to the Easter Hill study (see Cooper, 1975, p. 201) provides clear testimony to the need for longitudinal studies. The once exemplary housing project of Richmond has become, for many, a housing environment of last resort. Lack of maintenance, changes in the socioeconomic status of residents, and increases in the average number of inhabitants per dwelling unit have all undoubtedly contributed to the qualitative demise of Easter Hill. Different users bring with them different values and, quite likely, needs for a different kind of environment. Longitudinal studies, both person-centered and place-centered (see Chapter 1), can provide a basis for more-informed decisions on the design of new environments and the management of existing ones. Obviously, some postconstruction evaluations should also be viewed as baseline studies for monitoring over time.

CHAPTER EXERCISE

This activity involves selecting a recently built environment on or near your campus for study, one for which the designer (or the developer, if there was no designer) is known and available for an interview and one which is a public or quasi-public environment. Possible environments for study might include a plaza or mini-park, part or all of a new library, and social or circulation spaces of an academic building, student union, or shopping arcade. Have the class divide into teams. Each team will have responsibility for evaluating the environment using a different method—for example, open-ended interview, structured interview or questionnaire, observation, and check lists. An important first step for one team will be interviewing the designers or developer to obtain program information for standards and criteria.

Each team is to design the necessary responses and formats, define the required procedures (sampling, field operations, and so on) and apply them in the place being evaluated. *Note:* it may be necessary to obtain permission to conduct such studies in some places. The application can be in the form of a pretest that is intended to identify flaws in the study design and procedures and to make necessary corrections. The application should, however, be extensive enough so that the form of resulting data becomes apparent and questions of data analysis can be raised. Each team is to prepare a report on their part of the study so that comparisons can be made and discussions directed to questions such as:

1. What are the operational or in-the-field advantages and disadvantages of the various methods?
2. What kinds of data result from different methods: quantitative, qualitative, nominal, ordinal, interval, ratio?
3. In what ways do the different methods provide complementary or redundant information?
4. Should the collecting of redundant information be discouraged?
5. What were the specific benefits of conducting this pretest?
6. What kinds of analyses are appropriate for the different kinds of data?
7. Which methods would you finally select for this study? Why?
8. Were the standards and criteria that you identified adequate as a basis for evaluation?
9. If not, how could they have been improved?

SUPPLEMENTARY READINGS

The Friedmann, Zimring, and Zube book presents a systematic approach to evaluation and provides numerous illustrations of evaluation projects via case studies. The case studies include studies of interior space, single buildings, building complexes, and outdoor spaces. The emphasis is on methods and procedures. Sommer addresses two issues that are also primary topics of this book. The first half of his book considers the users of the built environment and their roles in design decision-making. The second half suggests ways to evaluate existing buildings and discusses how such evaluation data should be used in future designs.

Friedmann, A., Zimring, C., and Zube, E. *Environmental design evaluation.* New York: Plenum Press, 1978.
Sommer, R. *Design awareness.* San Francisco: Rinehart Press, 1972.

Chapter 8

POSTSCRIPT

TYING UP SOME LOOSE ENDS

The first four chapters of this book discussed the conceptual framework and background of public policy in relation to a user-based approach to environmental evaluation. The last three chapters presented case studies of actual evaluations. They were presented and analyzed within the conceptual framework or schema developed in the first four chapters. Furthermore, they served to illustrate the links, both weak and strong, between policy and evaluation.

The purpose of this final chapter is to review and restate some of the salient problems and issues that have been identified in the analysis of the eight case studies. The format for this review and restatement will parallel that of the case-study analyses—that is, it will follow the evaluation schema introduced in Chapter 1.

The case studies have not emphasized methods. That is not the intent of this book. There are, nevertheless, a number of methodological issues raised in the case studies that require further attention. For those readers interested in pursuing the topic of methods in greater detail, there are a number of useful recent references that address the use of behavioral science research methods in environmental studies in general (Lang, Burnette, Moleski, & Vachon, 1974; Michelson, 1975) and in postconstruction evaluation in particular (Sommer, 1972; Friedmann, Zimring, & Zube, 1978).

SOME INSTITUTIONAL ISSUES

Internalizing Evaluation

An important difference between pre- and postchange user-based studies is the greater tendency for the former to be internalized in the design process and the tendency of the latter to be ad hoc in nature and usually outside of the process. The implications of this difference are significant.

Prechange studies are frequently done by an agency staff or by consultants. When the cost and management are internalized, the primary purpose is usually to provide a qualitative subjective assessment to supplement more traditional quantitative physical-resource inventories or analyses of design alternatives. This qualitative user-assessment aids in defining problems and perceived solutions, identifying needs, and refining goals and objectives. In the case of qualitative inventories, such an assessment also provides baseline data for comparative evaluations of probable effects of proposed changes. The data generated by a design team or by their consultants are intended to be policy-relevant and to feed directly into the decision-making process involving policy-makers, administrators, design professionals, and citizen participants.

Ad Hoc Evaluations

The institutional aspects of postchange studies tend to be less clearly defined and more diffuse than is generally the case with prechange studies. While the purposes of postchange studies may be explicit with regard to assessing the success or failure of environments to resolve identified problems or to satisfy user needs, an explicit link to the design process is often unclear or nonexistent.

Inventories are recognized as an essential component of the early design process. While the notion of prechange user-based evaluations is relatively new, the idea of a quantitative and descriptive inventory and assessment of the existing physical environment is not. Quantitative inventory data are viewed as essential ingredients for design activities. In contrast, the notion of postchange evaluations and the specific concern with user-based evaluations is new, and has not been internalized in the design process. An important reason for this condition is that design budgets do not include funds for follow-up evaluations. And, when evaluation studies are undertaken with funding from some other source, the formal feedback loop of findings to the next iteration of a plan or design for a similar setting is tenuous at best.

Analyzing the Design Process

An important element in postconstruction evaluation is investigation of the design process. It should be obvious by now that the process is complex and involves many participants, and that many important decisions are made by individuals other than designers. The geographic location of a project, and its financing, may have been decided before a designer is involved. Furthermore, financing may be contingent on the inclusion of a specific number of rooms—for example, bedrooms or bathrooms in a house. The financing institution may be more concerned with resale value than with meeting the precise needs of the immediate occupant. In addition, zoning ordinances and building codes set further constraints. Thus, some aspects of the design that might contribute to user dissatisfaction, such as the undesirable location of a housing project within a community or the numbers and sizes of the rooms of individual housing units are not determined by user preferences, but, rather, by those building and financing the project and by state and local policies over which the designer may have little control.

SOME ENVIRONMENTAL PROBLEMS AND ISSUES

Domains, Taxonomies, and Physical Attributes

Three guidelines were given in Chapter 1 for a taxonomy of environmental domains. Briefly stated they are: (1) the taxonomy needs to be policy relevant; (2) the domains should be defined in terms of measurable physical elements, attributes, or characteristics; and (3) the domains need to be relevant to the perceptual/cognitive processes of user-participants. That there is no simple comprehensive environmental taxonomy with special relevance to perceptual/experiential evaluation is evident. This may be a reflection of the state-of-the-art, since research has not yet addressed this concern systematically, or it may be an indication that such a universal taxonomy is not feasible.

Nevertheless, studies undertaken thus far suggest that broad categories derived by planners and designers such as community, street, housing, or coastal zone—categories that might be found in a comprehensive taxonomy—are not adequate. Streets are classified according to traffic intensity. Housing is classified as detached house, rowhouse, or apartment, and could be further defined as high-rise apartment, garden apartment, and so on. And it is necessary to recognize the physical differences in the coastal zone.

Essentially, all of these categorizations are policy relevant and, as indicated previously, have been defined in physical terms. There is very little information, however, on the relevance of these or any other environmental taxonomies to participants' perceptual/cognitive processes. How do people describe their environments? For example, would a description or classification of streets as "light-traffic" or "heavy-traffic" be more meaningful to participants than classification as arterial street systems or local street systems? What is the psychological construct of the terms *street, house, community, forest,* or *rural?*

Most of the environmental taxonomies and related terms used in design are derived from the extensive experiences and technical vocabularies of professionals. They are compact and abstract representations of conditions or problems and encompass only that which is "essential or characteristic" (S. Kaplan, 1977, p. 223).

The importance of taxonomies and domain definitions relevant to the perceptual/cognitive processes of user-participants is central to the notion of perceptual/experiential evaluation as a part of the design process. Existing taxonomies represent efficient, short-hand ways in which large blocks of information are organized by professionals. For example, a residential classification of "R-1" in a given community can imply to the planner geographic location, lot size, building set-back requirements, house size, and available municipal services such as fire protection, water, and sewer. In addition, it can infer the socio-economic class of the residents. This one class of a land-use taxonomy is representative of all other land-use classes such as industrial, commercial or institutional in the amount of information it can convey to the professional. Considering that a land-use taxonomy can have three or more residential classifications, as well as multiple industrial, commercial, and institutional classifications, it abstracts an impressive amount of information for the professional—information that is usually not shared by user-participants involved in the evaluation process. This fact is particularly important in the evaluation of future environments discussed in Chapter 6.

Taxonomies are important in the design of instruments and procedures for evaluating existing environments. Such instruments and procedures should enhance communication between professionals and nonprofessionals, and explicitly recognize that laypersons are not familiar with the compact, abstract, organizing schema and vocabulary of the professional. If the findings from evaluation studies are to have a greater utility, it is important that a fit be found between the perceptions and experiences of user-participants and the information categories of the professionals, even if the latter have to be modified.

Explicit, user-relevant taxonomic and domain descriptions are also important to the fostering of comparisons among studies. Standardized taxonomies and evaluation instruments could provide for comparison among and aggregation of data from studies undertaken at the same time in different geographic locations and from studies undertaken at different times. The ability to generalize and develop predictive models could be enhanced considerably.

Design of Evaluation Studies—Measurement

The yardsticks or measures used in assessing the perceived quality of pre- and postchange environments are general and comparative. Rarely, if ever, are there absolute scales or measures. For example, evaluations may be accomplished by comparisons among several settings within the same domain, when the evaluative standards are implicit in the several settings being studied and the qualitative range is similarly limited and defined. The settings are ranked, or qualitatively ordered, according to aesthetic quality, satisfaction, or the like. Two general designs for the evaluation of multiple settings have been illustrated in the case studies. The first involves the evaluation of multiple settings (using photographic simulations), such as the aesthetic ranking of shoreline landscapes of the Virgin Islands, with each randomly selected participant evaluating all of the settings. Another design for multiple settings is illustrated by the visitor center and city streets studies, in which participants evaluated only the setting they were currently experiencing. The notion of generally equivalent groups used in the visitor center study recognizes the difficulty, if not impossibility, of random assignment of individuals to different environments such as housing, national parks, or city streets.

Another kind of yardstick or measure is exemplified by the Easter Hill study, in which the design program set forth assumptions about or criteria for the expected performance of an environment with regard to user satisfaction, behavioral patterns, use intensities, and kinds of users. Measurement was achieved by assessing the agreement or disagreement of perceptual/experiential responses with the program assumptions or criteria. The study of a single setting by a single group without a comparative reference can be useful for immediate decisions, such as in the building form and city park studies, but are usually of more limited policy-relevance.

A third approach, exemplified by the Belchertown State School study, compares perceptual/experiential responses to pre- and postchange conditions. The sequence of events in such a study is: (1) evaluation of existing environment; (2) change in existing environment; and, (3) evaluation of changed environment. The quality of the changed environment is determined by assessing the magnitude (how much) and the direction (positive or negative) of changes in user perceptions and experiences (behaviors) between the pre- and postchange conditions. The simplest design is one evaluation before the change and one after. The external validity of this approach—that is, the efficacy of generalizing to other settings and groups—can be enhanced, however, if multiple evaluations with multiple groups are employed (Campbell & Stanley, 1966, p. 40). Several evaluations before and after also help to account for the effects of time on perceptions and experiences.

A variation on the approach used in the BSS study presents a useful strategy for monitoring environmental quality. The primary difference in the environmental monitoring variation is that the intervention of a major change need not necessarily occur. The purpose of the monitoring might be simply to assess qualitative perceptual/experiential changes over time, relative to specific domains, changes that may be attributable to seemingly more modest modifications brought about by maintenance, overuse, different users, or new needs.

SOME PARTICIPATORY ISSUES

Who Participates

The most important participant issue is, simply, who is going to participate. As noted in Chapter 4, many of the traditional citizen-participation strategies are unsatisfactory for evaluation studies because they do not provide for representative participation. Representative participation, however, can sometimes be difficult to achieve, particularly in reference to planning inventories, evaluating alternative futures, and the evaluation of public areas and facilities. Strategies that have been employed range from random sampling to opportunity sampling.

Representative Samples

The U.S. Virgin Islands Coastal Zone study utilized a geographically stratified random sample. Geographic stratification was intended to provide minimum sample sizes within all subareas of the three major islands.

Similar strategies can be used in sampling for postchange studies. For example, buildings within a housing project can be grouped according to the kind of apartment units they contain (for example, studio, one-bedroom, two-bedroom), and a random sample can be selected such that the number of units sampled is proportional to the actual number of units in each building type. In drawing the sample at Easter Hill Village, however, Cooper (1975) selected a random sample without stratifying for building variability.

The question of stratification is obviously related to the kinds of analyses intended. If building type or style within a project or geographic subarea is hypothesized to be an important variable in resident satisfaction or aesthetic evaluation, stratification so as to provide a minimum number of respondents for each unit type is important.

Opportunity Samples

Opportunity samples were used in a number of the case studies, including the visitor center study. The costs of a random-sampling procedure for the twelve sites scattered between the Atlantic and Pacific coasts would have been prohibitive. Therefore, three days during peak-use season were selected for sampling users at each site. Retests conducted about six weeks later, during the peak season at two of the centers, indicated no significant differences in questionnaire or observation data.

There are obvious shortcomings in the use of opportunity samples—particularly with regard to the external validity or generalizability of the findings. Large numbers help somewhat to mitigate this limitation. Nevertheless, given the frequently encountered applied field-research limitations of time and/or money, valuable data, as was noted in our discussion of environmental sampling in Chapter 5, can be obtained from opportunity samples. Recognizing the limitations of the sample, the decision-maker still is provided with evaluative data that would not otherwise be available.

Nonusers

There is another kind of special group that merits attention, particularly in the evaluation of public places and facilities such as parks and open spaces—the nonusers. This group, however, is rarely considered. There are two major reasons why this is so. First, there is the factor of oversight or, according to the old adage, "out of sight, out of mind." The very terminology employed, "user-based evaluation," does not prompt one to think about nonusers. As a result, research instruments usually do not include questions or rating scales related to reasons for nonuse and nonusers' perceptions. The second reason is the difficulty of identifying nonusers. If a park evaluation study, for example, were designed as a random neighborhood household survey this would not be a problem. Random sampling procedures would protect against a biased sample and include both users and nonusers. But evaluations of such places are usually conducted at the site. Questionnaires are administered and observations conducted in the park, thus providing for better coordination in the use of multiple methods. In such a case, nonusers are effectively excluded from the evaluation. However, their perceptions of certain kinds of places and their reasons for not using them could be of considerable importance to decision-makers.

SOME THOUGHTS ON CLOSING THE POLICY/PRACTICE GAP

The policy/practice gap was defined in Chapter 2 as involving communications problems among participants in the planning process; different approaches to problem solving; decision-makers' concerns and doubts about the validity and reliability of social science data; the uneven state-of-the-art across domains; and the lack of institutionalized funding for evaluation studies. A significant thrust toward closing the gap was suggested by the development of standardized approaches, such as Perceived Environmental Quality Indices (PEQIs).

Among the hurdles to be crossed in the development and application of PEQIs, or of any other strategy for providing valid and reliable perceptual/experiential data to decision-makers, are those of comparability of findings across studies, common environmental taxonomies, and reliable sources of funding. Every time a new study is undertaken and a new instrument or procedure— questionnaire, interview, observation schedule, or rating scale—is devised without first asking if there is an already existing, tested, and reliable instrument, the problem of generalizing across studies is increased. Different instruments usually produce data that are not directly comparable. Obviously, studies vary and frequently have unique requirements. Nevertheless, there are also areas of commonality in many studies. Modular construction of instruments could, however, provide for both standard and unique parts of an instrument. The opportunity to analyze the effects of geographic or regional location, individual characteristics, and group characteristics on the perception of environmental quality could be extended considerably through the use of such standardized modular instruments. In the design of a specific study the researcher would select existing modules appropriate to the research and develop unique modules only where necessary.

Obviously, such cross-study aggregations and comparisons require a common environmental taxonomy as well, one that derives from the perceptual/cognitive processes of user-participants. Without a generally agreed on taxonomy, there is the very real possibility of aggregating or comparing evaluations of apples and zucchini squash—that is, of unique and noncomparable categories.

Progress toward closing the gap will continue to be uneven until funding patterns for evaluation studies are consciously addressed, perhaps by those agencies that have primary responsibility for specific domains and that come under the mandate of the National Environmental Policy Act. Programs in housing, parks and recreation, educational facilities, and transportation systems, as well as various functional planning activities, can be identified with specific agencies at the federal level. These agencies have their state and local counterparts that participate in these programs. This agency framework provides one potential avenue for the institutionalizing and funding of evaluation studies. Increased attention to needs for social science data, for funding for evaluation studies as a part of citizen-participation requirements, and for longitudinal studies could go a long way toward providing better social impact assessments and, in general, more valid and reliable information for decision-makers.

THE ROLE OF ACADEMIC INSTITUTIONS IN EVALUATION

A final note about the role of academic institutions in the area of environmental evaluation is, I believe, appropriate. Five of the case studies included in Chapters 5, 6, and 7 were done by university faculty and/or students: the city streets, visitor centers, Easter Hill, Belchertown State School, and city park studies. Easter Hill, recognized as an exemplary, if not a classic postconstruction evaluation study, was done as a masters degree thesis. The Belchertown State School study resulted in two Ph.D. dissertations and five masters theses.

Universities provide an important resource for advancing the art and science of environmental evaluations. Projects can be undertaken as course assignments by individuals or teams, as senior honors projects, masters theses or dissertations, and as faculty research activities. Furthermore, universities with academic programs in environmental planning and design could serve as regional resource centers for professionals and decision-makers requiring information on user-based evaluations, particularly in the area of post-construction evaluation. Also, universities can provide dynamic environmental simulation facilities, such as those found in the College of Environmental Design at Berkeley (McKechnie, 1977). Universities have both the intellectual skills and the library resources necessary to assist in closing the policy/practice gap.

SUPPLEMENTARY READINGS

In addition to the suggested supplementary readings for Chapter 7, which are related in part to methods used in post-construction evaluation, the following volumes address the more general issue of methods for environment and behavior research.

Lang, J., Burnette, C., Moleski, W., & Vachon, D. *Designing for human behavior*. Stroudsburg, Pa.: Dowden, Hutchinson and Ross, 1974.

Michelson, W. (Ed.), *Behavioral research methods in environmental design*. Stroudsburg, Pa.: Dowden, Hutchinson and Ross, 1975.

Zeisel, J. *Methodology and design in the environment and behavior field*. Monterey, Calif.: Brooks/Cole. (Forthcoming.)

REFERENCES

Abrams, C. *The city is the frontier*. New York: Harper & Row, 1965.

Altman, I. *The environment and social behavior*. Monterey, Calif.: Brooks/Cole, 1975.

American Falls International Board. *Preservation and enhancement of the American Falls at Niagara—appendix F: public involvement*. June 1974.

Appleyard, D. *Liveable urban streets: Managing auto traffic in neighborhoods*. Washington, D.C.: Superintendent of Documents, U.S. Government Printing Office, 1976.

Appleyard, D. Understanding professional media. In I. Altman and J. Wohlwill (Eds.), *Human behavior and environment*, vol. 2. New York: Plenum Press, 1977.

Babcock, L. R., Jr., & Nagda, N. L. Indices of air quality. In W. A. Thomas (Ed.), *Indicators of environmental quality*. New York: Plenum Press, 1972.

Battelle. *Measuring the social attitudes and aesthetic and economic considerations which influence transmission line routing*. Richland, Washington: 1974.

Berry, B. J. L., & Horton, F. E. *Urban environmental management*. Englewood Cliffs, N.J.: Prentice-Hall, 1974.

Bishop, A. B. Public participation in environmental impact assessment. In M. Bissett (Ed.), *Environmental impact assessment*. Engineering Foundation, 1976.

Boster, R. S., & Daniel, T. C. Measuring public responses to vegetative management. *Proceedings, 16th annual Arizona watershed symposium*. Phoenix: Arizona Water Commission, 1972, 38–43.

Cabot, J. B. *Supplementary visitor center information* (Reissue 1974). Unpublished manuscript, Denver Service Center, National Park Service, 1958.

Caldwell, L. K. *Environment: A challenge for modern society*. Garden City, N.Y.: The Natural History Press, 1970.

Campbell, A., Converse, P. E., & Rogers, W. L. *The quality of American life: perceptions, evaluations, and satisfactions*. New York: Russell Sage Foundation, 1976.

Campbell, D. T., & Stanley, J. C. *Experimental and quasi-experimental designs for research*. Chicago: Rand McNally, 1966.

Caplan, N., Morrison, A., & Stambaugh, R. J. *The use of social science knowledge in policy decisions at the national level*. Ann Arbor: Institute for Social Research, Univ. of Michigan, 1975.

Chadwin, M. L. The nature of legislative program evaluation. *Evaluation, 2*, 1975, 45–49.

Cook, T. D., & Campbell, D. T. The design and conduct of quasi-experiments and true experiments in field settings. In M. D. Dunnette (Ed.), *Handbook of industrial and organizational research*. Chicago: Rand McNally, 1975.

Coomber, N. H., & Biswas, A. K. *Evaluation of environmental intangibles*. Bronxville, N.Y.: Genera Press, 1973.

141

Cooper, C. C. *Easter Hill Village*. New York: The Free Press, 1975.

Cortner, H. A case analysis of policy implementation in the National Environmental Policy Act of 1976. *Natural Resources Journal, 16,* 323–338.

Coughlin, R. E., & Goldstein, K. A. *The extent of agreement among observers on environmental attractiveness*. Philadelphia: Regional Science Research Institute Discussion Paper 37, 1970.

Council on Environmental Quality, *Environmental quality, the seventh annual report of the council on environmental quality*. Washington, D.C.: Superintendent of Documents, U.S. Government Printing Office, 1976.

Craik, K. H., & Zube, E. H. *Issues in perceived environmental quality research*. Amherst, Mass.: Institute for Man and Environment, University of Massachusetts, 1975.

Craik, K. H., & Zube, E. H. *Perceiving environmental quality, research and applications*. New York: Plenum Press, 1976.

Daniel, T. C., & Boster, R. S. *Measuring landscape esthetics: The scenic beauty estimation method*. USDA Forest Service, Research Paper RM–167, Rocky Mountain Forest and Range Experiment Station, 1976.

Deane, D. C., & Mumpower, J. L. Social psychological level of analysis in social impact assessment. In K. Finsterbusch & C. P. Wolf (Eds.), *Methodology of social impact assessment*. Stroudsburg, Pa.: Dowden, Hutchinson & Ross, 1977.

Dearinger, J. A. *Esthetic and recreation potential of small naturalistic streams near urban areas*. Research Report No. 13. Lexington, Ky.: University of Kentucky, Water Resources Institute, 1968.

Eckbo, G. *The landscape we see*. New York: McGraw-Hill, 1969.

Finsterbusch, K. *A methodology for social impact assessments of highway locations*. Maryland Department of Transportation, State Highway Administration, Bureau of Research, 1976.

Finsterbusch, K., & Wolf, C. P. (Eds.). *Methodology of social impact assessment*. Stroudsburg, Pa.: Dowden, Hutchinson & Ross, 1977.

Friedmann, A., Zimring, C., & Zube, E. *Environmental design evaluation*. New York: Plenum Press, 1978.

Greenwood, N., & Edwards, J. M. B. *Human environments and natural systems*. North Scituate, Mass.: Duxbury Press, 1973.

Heberlein, T. A. Some observations on alternative mechanisms for public involvement: The hearing, public opinion poll, the workshop, and the quasi-experiment. *Natural Resources Journal. 16,* 1976, 197–212.

Heimstra, N. W., & McFarling, L. H. *Environmental psychology*. Monterey, Calif.: Brooks/Cole, 1978.

Jones & Jones. *Scenic and recreational highway study*. Seattle: For the Legislative Transportation Committee of Washington State, 1974.

Kaplan, R. The dimensions of the visual environment: Methodological considerations. In *Environmental design: Research and practice*. W. J. Mitchell (Ed.), Proceedings of the Environmental Design Research Association Conference Three, Los Angeles, 1972.

Kaplan, R. *Environmental design: The participation model*. (Photocopy) Ann Arbor: Department of Psychology, University of Michigan, 1973.

Kaplan, R. *Liberty Division Park: Citizen survey*. Report to the Ann Arbor Parks and Recreation Department, Michigan, January, 1976.

Kaplan, S. Participation in the design process: A cognitive approach. In D. Stokols (Ed.), *Perspectives on environment and behavior: Theory, research, and applications*. New York: Plenum Press, 1977.

Kaplan, S. *Concerning the power of content-identifying methodologies.* Paper presented at EDRA 9, Tucson, Arizona, April 10, 1978.

Kasperson, R. E., & Breitbart, M. *Participation, decentralization, and advocacy planning.* Resource Paper No. 25, Commission on College Geography. Washington, D.C.: Association of American Geographers, 1974.

Knight, R. C., Weitzer, W. H., & Zimring, C. M. *Opportunity for control and the built environment: The ELEMR project.* Amherst, Mass.: The Environmental Institute, University of Massachusetts, 1978.

Krueckeberg, D. A., & Silvers, A. L. *Urban planning analysis: Methods and models.* New York: John Wiley & Sons, 1974.

Lang, J., Burnette, C., Moleski, W., & Vachon, D. *Designing for human behavior.* Stroudsburg, Pa.: Dowden, Hutchinson & Ross, 1974.

Lansing, J. B., Marans, R. W., & Zehner, R. B. *Planned residential environments.* Ann Arbor: Institute for Social Research, University of Michigan, 1970.

Leopold, L. B. Landscape esthetics. *Natural History.* 1969, *78*, 36–45.

Marans, R. W., & Wellman, J. D. *The quality of nonmetropolitan living: Evaluations, behaviors and expectations of Northern Michigan residents.* Ann Arbor: Institute for Social Research, University of Michigan, 1978.

McKechnie, G. E. Simulation techniques in environmental psychology. In D. Stokols (Ed.), *Perspectives on environment and behavior theory, research and applications.* New York: Plenum Press, 1977.

Michelson, W. *Man and his urban environment: A sociological approach.* Reading, Mass.: Addison-Wesley, 1970.

Michelson, W. (Ed.). *Behavioral research methods in environmental design.* Stroudsburg, Pa.: Dowden, Hutchinson & Ross, Inc., 1975.

Morisawa, M. Evaluating riverscapes. In D. R. Coates (Ed.), *Environmental geomorphology, proceedings: First annual symposium.* Binghamton, N.Y.: State University of New York, 1971.

O'Riordan, T. Policy making in environmental management: Some thoughts on processes and research issues. *Natural Resources Journal.* 1976, *16*, 55–72.

Ostrander, E. The visual-semantic communication gaps. *Man-environment systems,* 1974, *4*, 47–53.

Palmer, J. F., & Zube, E. H. Numerical and perceptual landscape classification. In E. Zube (Ed.), *Studies in landscape perception.* Amherst: Institute for Man and Environment, University of Massachusetts, 1976.

Perfater, M. A. Comment on Llwellyn's analysis. In C. P. Wolf (Ed.), *Social impact assessment.* Washington, D.C.: Environmental Design Research Association, 1974.

Petula, J. M. *American environmental history.* San Francisco: Boyd & Fraser, 1977.

Porteous, J. D. *Environment and behavior: Planning and everyday urban life.* Reading, Mass.: Addison-Wesley, 1977.

Saarinen, T. F. *Environmental planning and behavior.* Boston: Houghton Mifflin, 1976.

Salasin, S. Experiment revisited: A conversation with Donald T. Campbell. *Evaluation.* 1973, *1*, 7–13.

Sax, J. L. *Defending the environment: A strategy for citizen action.* New York: Alfred A. Knopf, 1971.

Schomaker, J. H. Measurements of preferences for proposed landscape modifications. *Landscape Research.* 1978, 3:3, 5–9.

Shafer, E. L., Jr., & Mietz, J. Aesthetic and emotional experience rate high with northeast wilderness hikers. *Environment and Behavior.* 1969, *1*, 187–197.

Simon, H. A. *Administrative behavior.* New York: Macmillan, 1957.

Sochman, E. A. *Evaluative research*. New York: Russell Sage Foundation, 1967.

Sommer, R. *Design awareness*. Corte Madera, Calif.: Rinehart Press, 1972.

Sommer, R. Evaluation, yes: Research maybe. *Representative Research in Social Psychology*. 1973, *4*, 127–134.

U.S. Department of Commerce. *Social indicators 1976*. Washington, D.C.: Superintendent of Documents, U.S. Government Printing Office, 1977.

Virgin Islands Planning Office. *Public attitude survey, technical supplement no. 2*. Charlotte Amalie, St. Thomas: 1977a.

Virgin Islands Planning Office. *Preliminary program, Virgin Islands coastal zone management*. Charlotte Amalie, St. Thomas: 1977b.

Weinstein, N. Human evaluations of environmental noise. In K. H. Craik & E. H. Zube (Eds.), *Perceiving environmental quality, research and applications*. New York: Plenum Press, 1976.

White, E. T. *Introduction to architectural programming*. Tucson, Ariz.: Architectural Media, 1972.

Wilkinson, P. Public participation in environmental management: A case study. *Natural Resources Journal*. 1976, *16*, 117–135.

Wohlwill, J. Environmental aesthetics: The environment as a source of affect. In I. Altman & J. Wohlwill (Eds.), *Human behavior and environment, advances in theory and research, volume 1*. New York: Plenum Press, 1976.

Wohlwill, J. What belongs where: Research on fittingness of man-made structures in natural settings. *Landscape Research*. 1978, *3:3*, 3–5.

Wolf, C. P. (Ed.). *Social impact assessment*. Environmental Design Research Association, 1974.

Wolfensberger, W. *The principles of normalization in human services*. Toronto: National Institute on Mental Retardation, 1973.

Zeisel, J. *Methodology and design in the environment and behavior field*. Monterey, Calif.: Brooks/Cole. (Forthcoming.)

Zube, E. H. Perception of landscape and land use. In I. Altman & J. Wohlwill (Eds.), *Human behavior and environment, advances in theory and research, volume 1*. New York: Plenum Press, 1976.

Zube, E. H., Crystal, J. H., & Palmer, J. F. *Visitor center design evaluation*. Amherst: Institute for Man and Environment, University of Massachusetts, 1976.

Zube, E. H., & McLaughlin, M. Assessing perceived values of the coastal zone. In *Coastal zone 78*. New York: American Society of Civil Engineers, 1978.

Zube, E. H., Pitt, D. G., & Anderson, T. W. *Perception and measurement of scenic resources in the Southern Connecticut River Valley*. Amherst: Institute for Man and Environment, University of Massachusetts, 1974.

Zube, E. H., Pitt, D. G., & Anderson, T. W. Perception and prediction of scenic values of the northeast. In E. H. Zube, R. O. Brush, & J. G. Fabos (Eds.), *Landscape assessment: Values, perceptions and resources*. Stroudsburg, Pa.: Dowden, Hutchinson, & Ross, 1975.

INDEX